AWS Cloud Software Architecture
Interview Questions and Answers

Nova Trex

Contents

Preface

In the ever-evolving realm of technology, the cloud has emerged as a transformative force, reshaping industries and redefining the way we think about data and infrastructure. As businesses migrate to the cloud, the demand for professionals who can navigate this new frontier has surged. Among these roles, the Cloud Software Architect stands out as a beacon, guiding organizations through the intricacies of cloud design, deployment, and optimization. This book, "AWS Cloud Software Architecture: Interview Questions and Answers," is crafted to equip aspiring architects with the knowledge and confidence to excel in their interviews and embark on rewarding careers.

The cloud is not just a technological shift; it represents a paradigm change in how software is designed, deployed, and maintained. With AWS (Amazon Web Services) at the forefront of this revolution, understanding its nuances becomes paramount for any architect. This book delves deep into the heart of AWS, elucidating its components, best practices, and the architectural decisions that ensure scalable, reliable, and secure applications.

Structured as a series of questions and answers, this book offers readers a unique approach to learning. Each section is meticulously curated to cover a spectrum of topics, from the fundamental principles of cloud software architecture to the specifics of AWS. Whether you're a novice seeking foundational knowledge or a seasoned professional looking to brush up on advanced concepts, this book caters to every level of expertise.

As you journey through this book, remember that every interview is an opportunity to showcase your knowledge, passion, and vision. The questions and answers herein are not just to be memorized but understood, internalized, and applied. After all, the role of a Cloud Software Architect is not just about knowing the answers but about asking the right questions.

Welcome to "AWS Cloud Software Architecture: Interview Questions and Answers." Your path to mastering the cloud begins here.

Chapter 1

Introduction to Cloud Software Architecture

Cloud Software Architecture stands at the intersection of software development and modern infrastructure management, and this chapter seeks to unravel its intricate layers. Beginning with an exploration into the role of a Cloud Software Architect, we examine the scope, responsibilities, and challenges faced by professionals in this domain. It then transitions into an illuminating discussion on the foundational principles of Cloud Software Architecture, where concepts like scalability, microservices, and the importance of stateless components come under scrutiny. These principles not only guide the design of robust systems but also play a pivotal role in addressing common challenges such as latency and fault tolerance.

As we progress, the chapter pivots to a dedicated section on AWS Cloud Architecture, elucidating its significance in today's cloud-dominated landscape. From the shared responsibility model to the AWS Well-Architected Framework, this section offers a comprehensive overview of AWS's vast ecosystem and its contribution to building resilient, scalable, and cost-effective cloud solutions.

In sum, this chapter provides an encompassing introduction to the dynamic world of Cloud Software Architecture, setting the stage for deeper dives into subsequent topics.

1.1   Role of a Cloud Software Architect

The role of a Cloud Software Architect is both broad and complex, as it requires a mix of technical expertise, communication skills, and a solid understanding of business needs. This section introduces the responsibilities of a Cloud Software Architect and their vital role in the design and delivery of effective cloud solutions.

Cloud Software Architects are responsible for designing and implementing cloud-based applications. They are required to understand the technical requirements of the project, the capabilities and limitations of the cloud platform, as well as the business objectives that the project aims to achieve. Their tasks often involve making decisions about the appropriate cloud service model (IaaS, PaaS, SaaS), cloud deployment model (private, public, hybrid), and the specific cloud services or technologies to be used.

In addition to technical decisions, Cloud Software Architects are often also involved in managing stakeholder expectations, coordinating with project teams, and ensuring the scalability, security, and cost-efficiency of the solutions they design.

A competent Cloud Software Architect requires a deep understanding of cloud computing technology, excellent problem-solving skills, and the ability to translate business requirements into technological solutions. With the increasing adoption of cloud technologies, the role of a Cloud Software Architect has become crucial in modern software development and deployment.

What are the main responsibilities of a Cloud Software Architect?

A Cloud Software Architect plays a crucial role in designing and managing the cloud-based systems within an organization. Their job involves not just structuring the technical aspects, but also understanding the business side and deliver solutions that is the best fit for their company's mission and strategy.

Here are some of the main responsibilities of a Cloud Software Architect:

1. **Strategic Decision Making**: The Cloud Software Architect must make strategic decisions about the adoption of cloud technologies, deciding to use different service models (IaaS, PaaS, SaaS), the cloud deployment models (private, public, hybrid, or multi-cloud) based on the business needs and the technological context.

2. **Designing of Cloud Environment and Applications**: Once the strategic decisions are made, the Cloud Software Architect is responsible for designing the abstract and physical layers of a cloud environment, including the applications, APIs, front-end platforms, back-end platforms, servers, storage, and delivery networks.

3. **Integration and Middleware**: The architect should ensure the integration of the designed cloud architecture with the current environment (if applicable). This involves dealing with middleware systems that interconnect different software modules and/or services.

4. **Security and Compliance**: The architect should also ensure that the cloud services are compliant with corporate and/or legal policies. They are responsible for security design, risk mitigation, and disaster recovery planning.

5. **Performance and Optimization**: The Cloud Software Architect is responsible for defining the Key Performance Indicators (KPIs) and ensuring that the cloud system is performing at its optimal capability.

6. **Governance and Operational Excellence**: The Cloud Software Architect develops the governance strategy and policies, guides the organization towards operational excellence, and encourages a culture of efficiency and continuous improvement.

It's worth noting, that the mix of these responsibilities might vary based on the company's size, domain, and business needs. For example, in a health-care company, Security and Compliance (*SC*) might be given more weight than in other industries.

How do you balance business requirements with technical constraints as a Cloud Architect?

Balancing business requirements with technical constraints is often a challenging aspect of being a Cloud Software Architect. This duty demands a comprehensive understanding of both the business needs and the technical landscape. The architect has to align technologies to serve business goals while ensuring efficiency, security, and cost-effectiveness.

One way to achieve this balance is following these steps:

Understanding Business Objectives: The Cloud Architect's role starts with a profound understanding of the business objectives. This understanding provides the context in which all architectural decisions are made and helps ensure that the technology serves the business. For example, if cost-saving is a major objective, the architect might choose a multi-tenant architecture on a platform like AWS, to optimize resource usage and reduce costs.

Assessing Technical Constraints: A deep understanding of available technologies, resources, and their limitations is also vital. Is the existing codebase compatible with the desired cloud platform? Are there specific compliance or regulatory requirements? Is there a preferred programming language? Do we have the necessary skills in-house? All of these questions help shape the technical constraints.

Building a Bridging Strategy: The understanding of business objectives and technical constraints allows a Cloud Architect to build strategies that bridge them effectively. This might mean compromising in some areas or innovating in others. For example, if an application is currently in a programming language that is not supported by AWS Lambda, a solution could be to use a compatibility layer, do a partial or complete code rewrite, or use a different AWS service instead of Lambda.

Communication and Collaboration: The Cloud Architect liaises between the technical and business sides, explaining clearly why certain decisions had been taken, what compromises may have been made, and what the implications are. Collaboration here is vital; working with stakeholders on both sides leads to better mutual understanding and better, more balanced solutions.

The 'Balanced Solution' area — the intersection of the 'Business requirements' and 'Technical constraints' circles — represents the optimal solutions that successfully align the business needs with the available technical capabilities.

How do you approach cost management in cloud architecture?

The cost management in cloud architecture requires a comprehensive approach that includes cost monitoring, cost optimization, and cost allocation. As an architect, your role includes exercising resource efficiency, scenario modeling, and budget enforcement to prevent unnecessary cloud spending.

Cost Monitoring

To manage costs effectively, you need to first monitor and track them. AWS provides tools like Cost Explorer and AWS Budgets for this. Cost Explorer allows you to view and analyze your costs and usage. AWS Budgets, on the other hook, tracks your AWS usage and costs, and can alert you when your budget thresholds are breached.

Cost Optimization

Once you have a clear understanding of where your money is going, your next objective should be to reduce costs where possible. This is where architectural decisions made by a cloud software architect can make a significant difference. Here are a few strategies that you may employ:

1. **Right Sizing:** You should ensure that you are using the right type and number of resources. AWS provides a plethora of options with varying capabilities and costs. By understanding the requirements and patterns of the applications you can choose the most cost effective options.

2. **Elasticity:** One of the biggest benefits of cloud is the ability to scale up or down based on demand. You can set up Auto Scaling so that you only pay for what you need.

3. **Choosing the right pricing model:** AWS offers options like Savings Plans or Reserved Instances that provide significant savings if you can commit to a certain level of usage.

4. **Storage Optimization:** You should also pay attention to storage costs which can be a significant part of your bill. S3 Intelligent-Tiering is an AWS feature that helps save costs by automatically moving data between different storage classes based on usage patterns.

Cost Allocation

Attributing costs to the right departments or projects is important for accountability. AWS provides tagging which allows you to organize your resources and apply cost allocation tags. The Cost Allocation Report, then provides visibility of costs by these tags.

Scenario Modeling

AWS provides the AWS Pricing Calculator which allows you to estimate costs. You can put together different scenarios and see the cost implications. This is particularly useful in making architectural decisions, or when making significant changes to your configurations.

In conclusion, cost management involves continuous monitoring and ongoing optimization efforts. As a cloud architect, understanding the cost implications of architectural decisions is a key part of the role.

How do you ensure cloud-based systems are scalable and reliable?

Ensuring the scalability and reliability of cloud-based systems is a vital role for a cloud software architect. Here are a few strategies to achieve it:

1. Design for Scalability: The architecture should support horizontal scaling, which means adding more machines to the network to handle increased load. AWS offers Auto Scaling service that automatically adjusts capacity to maintain steady, predictable performance at the lowest possible cost.

$$Scaling = \frac{traffic\,increase}{capacity\,increase}$$

This equation simply means that the ability to scale (i.e., scalability) equals the rate of traffic increase divided by the rate of capacity increase. The closer the ratio is to 1, the better the system is capable of scaling. If it's less than 1, it means the system is not scaling sufficiently to handle the increased traffic.

2. Design for Failover: Architectures should be designed in a way to handle system or component failures. This can be achieved by incorporating redundancy and automatic failover into the system. With AWS, you can use services like Amazon Route 53 which is designed to enable low-latency DNS routing to improve service availability. Similarly, AWS offers Elastic Load Balancing which automatically distributes incoming application traffic across multiple targets.

3. Design for High Availability: The architecture should be designed

to minimize downtime and service disruption. In AWS, we can spread load across different AWS Availability Zones in a region. Each Availability Zone runs on its own physically distinct, independent infrastructure and is engineered to be highly reliable.

4. Design for Disaster Recovery: AWS offers services like AWS Backup for automated backup services and AWS Elastic Disaster Recovery for the recovery of services in the event of a disaster.

5. Smoothing the Load: Unexpected peaks in traffic can bring down a system. Implementing a queue can smooth out these peaks by buffering incoming requests. AWS SQS (Simple Queue Service) can be used to manage and decouple these messages.

6. Monitoring and Logging: CloudWatch and X-Ray are services offered by AWS to monitor the system. It helps identify potential problems before they have any adverse effects.

Let's take a look at an example of designing for high availability:

$$Availability = \frac{Uptime}{Uptime + Downtime}$$

Assume that we have 99.95% availability for each individual EC2 instance:

$$0.9995 = \frac{Uptime}{Uptime + Downtime}$$

If we use the Multi-AZ model in AWS where two instances run in parallel in separate Availability Zones, the unavailability of both at the same time will be the product of their individual unavailabilities:

$$Unavailability\,(Multi-AZ) = Unavailability\,(Zone\,1) * Unavailability\,(Zone\,2)$$
$$= (1 - 0.9995) * (1 - 0.9995)$$

So, the availability increases:

$$Availability = 1 - Unavailability\,(Multi - AZ)$$

Therefore, it is evident that by using diversified resources and redundancy, we can ensure a higher level of availability and reliability in the cloud environment.

What is your process for staying up-to-date with new cloud technologies and best practices?

As an AWS Cloud Software Architect, staying up-to-date with new cloud technologies, updates, best practices, and emerging trends is crucial to provide clients with the best possible solutions. A systematic approach to continuous learning might include the following steps:

1. **Continual Education Opportunities**: Taking advantage of continual education through AWS Training and Certification courses, such as 'Architecting on AWS' & 'Advanced Architecting on AWS', can help to familiarize with new services and features.

2. **AWS News Blogs & AWS Whitepapers**: They are authoritative sources of new AWS services, notable updates, architectural best practices, and strategies for dealing with common problems. They provide deep dives into technical details and are updated frequently.

3. **Participation in AWS Events/Conferences**: Participation in events like AWS re:Invent, AWS Summits, and online webinars can provide access to the latest AWS developments. These opportunities also facilitate learning directly from the AWS team and allow for networking with other cloud professionals.

4. **Online Communities & Forums**: Participating in online AWS communities, LinkedIn groups, and forums can provide both knowledge gain and knowledge sharing opportunities. Websites like StackOverflow, AWS discussion forums, and GitHub can provide further insights.

5. **Hands-on Experience**: Regularly experimenting with the AWS Free Tier, to actually use new technologies, features, and see their outcomes. This also provides practical experience of the pros and cons of those features, rather than just theoretical understanding.

6. **Revising AWS Well-Architected Framework**: This framework gives a set of best practices and strategies to follow which are updated from time to time. Revising it periodically is suggested.

7. **Subscribing to Newsletters**: Newsletters from AWS, third-party cloud consultancies, and tech publications can also provide knowledge of trends and developments.

8. **Follow Thought Leaders**: Following AWS cloud thought leaders on social media platforms to get insights on cutting-edge implementations and use cases.

Just as cloud technology is continually evolving, so should our understanding and knowledge of it. Remaining up to-date-requires regular effort but offers substantial rewards in terms of effectiveness and success in the role of a Cloud Software Architect.

How do you handle security concerns in a cloud architecture?

Handling security concerns as a Cloud Software Architect in AWS (Amazon Web Service) typically involves a multi-level approach that addresses every level of the cloud architecture. Herein lies the central principle of "Security at all levels".

1. **Identity and Access Management (IAM)**:

Cloud Software Architect must ensure that only authorized and authenticated users can access your data and resources. This can be accomplished through AWS Identity and Access Management (IAM) which controls access to AWS services and resources securely. For example, you could create an IG (Identity Group) for each department (like HR, IT, Admin) and restrict their access accordingly.

IAM : Secure → Authorized Users → Restricted Access → (to) Services/Resources

2. **Secure Network Architecture**:

Another aspect is to set up a secure network architecture. This includes setting up Security Groups and Access Control Lists (ACLs) to allow only necessary traffic to your instances. For example, you can configure a security group to allow traffic only from known IP addresses.

3. **Data Encryption**:

Encrypting data at rest and in transit adds another layer of defense. AWS provides several services for this purpose like AWS Key Management Service (KMS), AWS CloudHSM, etc. As an example, using Amazon S3 Server-side encryption (SSE) you can automatically encrypt objects at rest.

Data Encryption → KMS/CloudHSM → Transit/At Rest → Automatic Encryption (SSE)

4. **Detective Control**:

Another technique is to employ detective control like using AWS CloudTrail, Amazon CloudWatch, AWS Config to collect and analyze logs for any abnormalities or patterns that may indicate suspicious activity.

5. **Infrastructure protection**:

On the infrastructure level, in AWS, you can protect your VPCs (Virtual Private Cloud) with security groups, implement hostile and inbound traffic analysis with Shield and WAF (Web Application Firewall).

6. **Incident Response**:

In case a security incident happens, you need to have a recovery plan. AWS provides services like AWS CloudEndure Disaster Recovery, which ensures business continuity by keeping your applications available all the time.

Incident Response → Data Breach → Recovery Plan
   → CloudEndure Disaster Recovery → Business Continuity

Remember the important principle, shared responsibility model by AWS "Security OF the cloud is the responsibility of AWS and security IN the cloud is the responsibility of the customer".

To summarize, handling security concerns in a cloud architecture is a top-to-bottom process, that extends from making sure identity and access are carefully managed to setting up disaster recovery planning. Following best practices in this process drastically reduces the risk of security incidents.

Can you describe a time when you had to make a tough decision about the architecture of a system? What was the outcome?

Let's say we are working on a project having a microservices architecture running on AWS. The application is experiencing high latency issues and we need to find a solution quickly. The architecture consists of five different services running in different Amazon EC2 instances, and an Amazon RDS DB instance where all data is stored. To diagnose the latency, we use CloudWatch, AWS's monitoring and observability service.

The issue is found to be with the database service. It is a monolithic DB handling all the services, hence causing a bottleneck. Now we have a critical decision to make. Should we continue using a single RDS instance with a stronger instance type, or should we shift the architecture to use Amazon DynamoDB, a NoSQL database service offered by AWS?

Taking the first option would be easy on the development side since we just need to migrate to a bigger instance. However, the financial team is not supporting this solution since this will considerably increase costs.

The second option: Transitioning into using DynamoDB requires a substantial codebase change. Our development team needs time to rewrite and test parts of our code. But this will result in more scalable architecture and may solve the latency issue in the long-term without requiring continuous upgrade of our instances.

This decision requires a deep understanding of both the business and technical aspects. We must balance short-term and long-term impacts, budget, and feasibility. Assuming we choose to move to DynamoDB, the architecture would change to look like this:

- Each microservice will have its own DynamoDB table(s)

- Direct interaction with DB is avoided and instead services communicate through API calls

- Amazon SNS and SQS can be used for decoupling and to maintain loose coupling.

This decision would provide scalability, performance, and cost efficiency in the long run, despite the heavy initial development tasks needed.

These are the types of decisions Cloud Architects deal with while working amidst often conflicting interests in real-world projects. The critical skills in such situations are the ability to take a holistic view, the understanding of long-term impacts of decisions, and clear communication with stakeholders.

How do you approach communicating technical details to non-technical stakeholders?

Effective communication with non-technical stakeholders requires a Cloud Software Architect to be able to convey complex cloud architecture and flow of operations in a simpler, business-centric manner.

Here are some strategies:

1. **Avoid Jargon:** Ensure you are avoiding technical jargon as much as possible. Made-up example: Instead of saying "We're going to implement a containerized microservices architecture on a Kubernetes-managed cluster in AWS", you might say "We are going to arrange our software in small, manageable pieces which can be easily updated without disrupting the entire system. We're going to use recognized approaches and tools in the industry that will manage these pieces efficiently."

2. **Use Analogies:** Explain complex cloud concepts using simple real-world analogies. For example, explaining a distributed system using the analogy of a team working on different parts of a project in different locations, still synchronized to meet the project objectives.

3. **Visual Diagrams:** These are your best friend in explaining complex architecture. AWS provides some guided tools like AWS Architecture Diagrams allowing you to create designs, charts, and diagrams for visual representation. From load balancers to database instances, simply display how each component interacts with the other.

4. **Explain Benefits:** Focus on the business benefits, use case, and outcomes rather than the technical details. Like how a particular architecture makes the system more scalable or more reliable.

5. **Simplify Concepts with User Story or Use Cases:** Explaining with the context of how the end user will interact with the system can simplify technical complexities. For instance, explaining the role of a cache by discussing how it reduces waiting time for a frequent user.

Please remember that the role of a Cloud Software Architect is not only about having technical expertise, but it requires strong communication skills to effectively relay this information to non-technical stakeholders.

How do you manage and mitigate risks in cloud architecture?

Managing and mitigating risks in cloud architecture is vitally important to ensure a smooth run of applications and services while maintaining a high level of security and accessibility. A Cloud Software Architect must execute a series of tasks, including, but not limited to, the following:

1. **Risk Identification**: The first step in risk management is identifying potential risk. These could include security breaches, data loss, availability guarantees, compliance violations, and potential system or vendor failures.

2. **Risk Analysis**: After identifying risks, the next step is to conduct a thorough risk analysis. Each risk should be quantified in terms of its potential impact, the likelihood of its occurrence, and the cost of its mitigation.

The formula for risk quantification is:

$$Risk = Likelihood(L) \times Impact(I)$$

where:

- Likelihood is the probability of the risk occurring. This can be estimated as a percentage.

- Impact is the consequences if the risk were to happen. This could include costs (like downtime, loss of customers, or fines), and is usually measured in financial terms.

3. **Risk Prioritization**: Based on the quantified risks, they should be prioritized in terms of their potential impact and the immediacy of their threat. This creates a risk priority list.

4. **Risk Mitigation**: High priority risks must be addressed first. Different mitigation strategies may be employed, including accepting

the risk (when the cost of mitigation exceeds the potential damage), mitigating the risk (reduce the likelihood and/or impact), transferring the risk (such as insurances), or avoiding the risk (change the system design).

5. **Risk Monitoring and Review**: Risk management is a continuous process. Prioritized risks should be regularly reviewed and monitored to ensure that mitigation strategies are still effective and necessary.

For example, an enterprise might use AWS services, where data breaches can be a potential risk. To mitigate this, the Cloud Software Architect could design a system implementing encryption of all data both in transit and at rest, using AWS Key Management Service or AWS CloudHSM for key management. AWS's Identity and Access Management (IAM) allows control of who is authenticated and authorized to use resources, reducing the risk of unauthorized data access.

All these risk management strategies are interconnected and iterative in nature. Being proactive in managing risks can prevent or minimize their impact on the business, which is why it is such a critical part of the role of a Cloud Software Architect.

To clearly present these risk management process, the following graphic illustrates steps:

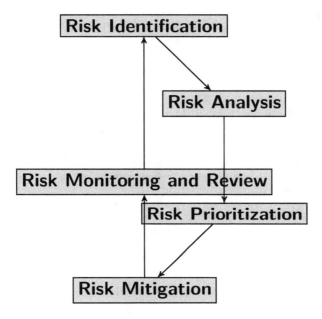

With the rising adoption of cloud-based services, risk management is becoming paramount for any organization to shield itself from potential damage.

Can you discuss your experience with disaster recovery planning in cloud architecture?

Cloud software architects should be proficient in understanding, analyzing, designing, and implementing a well-orchestrated disaster recovery (DR) plan. In AWS, there are several tools and services that can be used to automate and orchestrate DR strategies. These include AWS Lambda, Amazon EC2, Amazon S3, Amazon RDS, Amazon DynamoDB, Amazon Route53, AWS CloudFormation, to mention a few.

The DR planning revolves around four major strategies:

- **Backup & Restore:** In this strategy, data is regularly backed up to Amazon S3, which provides high durability. The backed-up data can be restored when required. This strategy is more economically feasible because the operations are not performed regularly, but this comes at the expense of a longer Recovery Time Objective (RTO).

- **Pilot Light:** In this strategy, a minimal version of an environment is always maintained in the AWS cloud. In case of a disaster, this environment is thoroughly configured to handle the full load. Even though the recovery time is less than the Backup & Restore strategy, maintaining the minimal version may incur cost.

- **Warm Standby:** Here, a scaled-down version of a fully functional environment is always running in the cloud. During a disaster, the system can be quickly ramped up to handle the full load. This strategy ensures a quicker recovery time, but it involves higher costs due to the running state of duplicate resources.

- **Multi-Site:** This is the most robust and costly DR strategy. In this strategy, an organization runs duplicate environments in multiple AWS regions. This will provide the quickest recovery time in case of disasters, but the cost is significantly high due to the continuous running of duplicate environments.

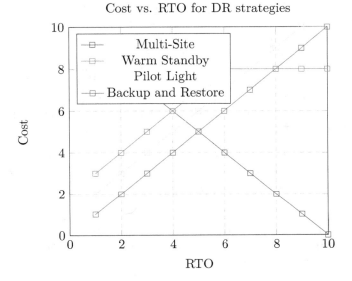

Cost vs. RTO for DR strategies

The graph provides a conceptual view of how cost and RTO vary for these DR strategies. The choice of strategy depends on the tolerance of the business for downtime (RTO) and data loss (RPO), balanced against the costs of preparing for & recovering from a disaster.

Considering the importance of disaster recovery planning, a cloud software architect plays a crucial role in designing a highly available, fault-tolerant, and secure cloud system on AWS. The primary goal is to ensure that essential data is safe and applications stay online, even when confronted with a catastrophic event.

1.2   Fundamental   Principles   of   Cloud Software Architecture

This section delves into the fundamental principles that underpin cloud software architecture. These principles set a foundation for how systems are designed and deployed on the cloud, ensuring that the applications are scalable, reliable, and secure.

Among the key principles discussed include the shared responsibility model, a cornerstone of cloud computing that divides security responsibilities between the cloud service provider and the customer. The principle of elasticity, which refers to the ability of cloud systems to adapt to changes in workload by automatically scaling resources up or down, is another fundamental concept in cloud architecture.

Design for failure is another critical principle. In cloud software architecture, systems must be designed to handle failure without suffering significant downtime or data loss, making concepts like redundancy and fault-tolerance key.

Security is a paramount principle in cloud software architecture. Given that data is hosted on third-party servers, cloud applications need robust security measures to protect sensitive information from cyber threats.

Finally, cost optimization is an integral principle of cloud software architecture. Given that one of the key advantages of cloud computing is its pay-as-you-go model, architects must design systems to maximize efficiency and control costs. This involves selecting the right services, configuring them correctly, and continuously monitoring usage and performance.

What are the five pillars of the AWS Well-Architected Framework?

The AWS Well-Architected Framework provides a consistent approach for customers and partners to evaluate architectures, and implement designs that can scale over time. The AWS Well-Architected Framework is based on five pillars:

Operational Excellence - This pillar focuses on running and monitoring systems to deliver business value, and continually improving processes and procedures.

Security - This pillar involves protecting information, systems. Key topics include confidentiality and integrity of data, identifying and managing who can do what with privilege management, protecting systems, and establishing controls to detect security events.

Reliability - This pillar involves ensuring a workload performs its intended function correctly and consistently when it's expected to. A resilient workload quickly recovers from failures to meet business and customer demand.

Performance Efficiency - This pillar focuses on using IT and computing resources efficiently. Key topics include selecting the right resource types and sizes based on workload requirements, monitoring performance, and making informed decisions to maintain efficiency as business needs evolve.

Cost Optimization - This pillar focuses on avoiding unnecessary costs. Key topics include understanding and controlling where money is being spent, selecting the most appropriate and right number of resources types, analyzing spend over time, and scaling to meet business needs without overspending.

These five pillars form the basis on which other well-architected aspects of Cloud Computing (like planet-friendly architectures or data management) are placed, and help organizations apply best practices for designing and managing their cloud architectures.

In fact, the AWS Well-Architected Framework is often depicted as a diagram, where each of the five pillars forms one part of the supporting structure underneath the "workload" (i.e., your software architecture) that's being put onto the cloud.

What is a loosely coupled system and why is it important in cloud architecture?

Loosely coupled system is a key concept in software architecture, especially in the context of cloud computing. Essentially, a loosely coupled system refers to a design principle where the components (or services) of a system can interact without (or with minimal) dependencies on each other.

Loose coupling has several advantages which make it ideal for cloud architecture.

1. **Scalability:** Loosely coupled services can be scaled independently according to demand. For instance, if a service A is experiencing high demand, we can create more instances of A without affecting service B.

2. **Fault isolation:** In a loosely coupled system, if one component fails, it won't take the whole system down with it. This property is crucial to maintaining system availability.

3. **Ease of development and maintenance:** Having independent components means they can be developed, updated, or replaced without impacting the others.

4. **Better load distribution:** Loosely coupled components can be distributed across different servers or geographical locations to better manage the load and decrease latency.

In cloud architecture, loosely coupled systems are often realized through the use of microservices architecture, where each microservice is a small, independent component that communicate with each other via well-defined APIs. Although adopting such an architecture could add complexity to the system design and need careful coordination, the benefits provided in terms of scalability, resilience, and flexibility make it an attractive choice for cloud software developers.

Can you explain the concept of stateless design?

Stateless design is a critical principle in cloud software architecture. The central idea behind a stateless design is that a server does not need to keep track of any information or "state" about its clients. Instead, each request is handled independently of any other requests.

This design principle is fundamental in achieving scalability and reliability in a cloud environment for the following reasons:

1. **Horizontal Scaling:** Stateless applications can be quickly scaled horizontally by simply adding more instances as each instance is independent of the others. No information sharing is required among its distributed instances, making the scaling process easier and more efficient.

2. **Simplicity and predictability:** Stateless design reduces the complexity of application development since developers don't have to deal with synchronization, shared memory, and related concurrency issues. Each request is handled independently which makes it much more simple and predictable.

3. **Fault Tolerance and Reliability:** In a stateless design, if an application process crashes, it does not impact the client's interaction because no session information (state) is lost. Future requests from the client can be handled by any other running application process.

In a web application, for example, this design principle would imply that no client session data is stored on the server. Instead, all session data is stored on the client-side, and the server uses a token to authenticate each client request without needing to remember any prior request.

However, it's worth noting that the stateless design doesn't mean no state at all. Instead, it separates the concern of storing the state from the backend tiers of the application and introduces a state tier in the architecture.

The following is a simple example of stateless server interaction:

- Client (C1) sends request (R1) to the server (S1).

- Server (S1) processes request (R1) and returns response (RE1) to the client (C1).

- The server (S1) does not keep a record of this transaction.

Here is a simple diagram representing this interaction.

```
C1 ----R1----> S1
C1 <---RE1---- S1
```

In terms of implementation on AWS, AWS Lambda is an excellent example of stateless design. Each execution of your Lambda function is independent. The developer does not need to worry about the state of the application, AWS Lambda handles it all.

How does elasticity differ from scalability in cloud computing?

Elasticity and scalability are both key principles in cloud software architecture and they are often used interchangeably. However, they have different meanings.

Elasticity is the ability for the cloud service to quickly adapt to changes in workload demands by dynamically adding or withdrawing resources as required. With elasticity, resources can be automatically scaled up or down depending on the demand at any given time. This ensures that the system always has the necessary resources to perform optimally, and it can be crucial in situations where workloads are unpredictable or highly variable.

Scalability, on the other hand, is the ability of a system to handle increases in load by increasing the capacity of the system. This means that as the demand or workload on the system increases, additional resources (CPU, memory, storage, etc.) can be added to the system to meet the increased demand. Scalability can be either vertical (adding more power to an existing machine) or horizontal (adding more machines to the system).

In essence, while both elasticity and scalability deal with the system's ability to handle differing amounts of workload, the key difference lies in the time dimension. Scalability is a long term strategy, usually planned and executed over longer periods. Elasticity, however, is a short term, real-time response to immediate changes in demand.

As an example, consider a retail company 'A' during the holiday period. To cope with the long-term, sustained increase in demand during this period, they might use scalability strategies like adding servers to their infrastructure. But, within this period, there could be spikes in traffic on a day-to-day or even minute-to-minute basis (e.g., flash sales), and to handle this variable demand, they would rely on the elasticity of their system.

In other words, scalability helps 'A' prepare their systems for the holiday period, and elasticity helps them handle the sudden surges in traffic efficiently and cost-effectively. Without either, they risk downtimes, poor performances, and added costs from over-provisioning resources.

Can you explain the concept of "Infrastructure as Code" (IaC)?

In cloud-based software architecture, "Infrastructure as Code" (IAC) is a key principle that refers to the process of managing and provisioning computing infrastructure with machine-readable definition files, rather than physical hardware configuration or interactive configuration tools.

In traditional settings, the server infrastructure might include large amounts of configuration changes that are made manually - a process that is time-consuming, risks human error, and is not easily scalable.

IaC represents a shift in the way infrastructure is managed, bringing in benefits like speed, replicability, and syncing with version control systems like GIT.

For example, rather than manually setting up a server by installing operating system, configuring your network, setting up your database, and then running your application, you'd use IaC to define all these settings in, for example, an AWS CloudFormation template. You can then take this template and create identical copies of this infrastructure at a click of a button, with no room for human error or manual mistakes. This allows teams to spend more time building product features and less time managing infrastructure.

Examples of tools and services for IaC include:

- AWS CloudFormation

- Google Cloud Deployment Manager

- Azure Resource Manager

- Terraform

- Chef, Puppet, and Ansible for configuration management

Here's an example of an AWS CloudFormation syntax for an S3 bucket:

```
"Resources" : {
  "S3Bucket" : {
    "Type" : "AWS::S3::Bucket",
    "Properties" : {
      "BucketName" : "MyBucket"
    },
    "DeletionPolicy" : "Retain"
  }
}
```

This JSON code specifies that we want to create a resource of type AWS::S3::Bucket, and we're naming the bucket "MyBucket". If this infrastructure needs to be deleted, the policy we've set ("Retain") ensures the bucket will not be deleted.

In the context of DevOps, IaC can be utilized to develop and change infrastructure faster and more efficiently. By pairing IaC with version control systems, continuous integration (CI) tools, and automated testing tools, a complete view of releases and changes can be tracked and managed, just like any other software.

Why is it important to design for failure in cloud computing?

Designing for failure in cloud computing is crucial because in the cloud, failures are inevitable. The cloud is composed of countless components, including servers, virtual machines, networks, storage devices, and other infrastructure components. It's statistically impossible for all of these components to work perfectly at all times. Therefore, we need to expect that some of them will fail at any given moment, and we need to architect our systems to endure such failures without causing significant disruptions to our services. This is why designing for failure is a fundamental principle of cloud software architecture.

In practical terms, designing for failure in the cloud involves strategies like:

1. **Redundancy:** Duplicating critical components of the system to ensure continuous service even when one component fails. For example, we could run multiple instances of a web server and use a load balancer to distribute traffic across them.

2. **Fault Isolation and Bulkheads:** Partitioning a system into isolated components to limit the extent of possible failure. A failure in one component should not lead to systemic failures.

3. **Use of Health Checks:** Implementing automated routines that monitor the health of the application, so that failures can be detected and fixed promptly.

4. **Stateless Design of Components:** Designing components to not maintain any internal state. This means if a component fails, another can easily take over its responsibility without loss of service.

5. **Circuit Breakers Pattern:** This prevents a failure from continuously occurring and cascading throughout the system. It's like an automatic switch that halts the failure's propagation.

The mathematical reliability theory shows that systems with redundancy have higher reliability than systems without. If we denote:

- R_1 as the reliability of a system with no redundancy,
- R_n for a system with n redundant components (and $n \geq 1$),
- R as the reliability of an individual component,

then we have:

$R_1 = R$, and,

$R_n = 1 - (1 - R)^{n+1}.$

As R_n increases with n, it's clear that redundancy improves system reliability.

This can be visualised graphically, where the x-axis represents the number of redundant components and the y-axis represents system reliability.

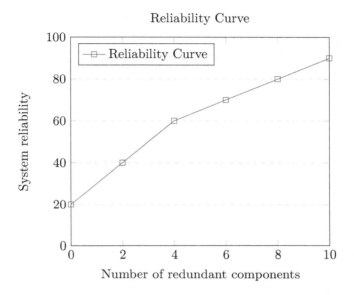

In conclusion, by designing for failure, we can improve the reliability, availability, and resilience of our cloud applications. This leads to improved customer satisfaction and trust, increased productivity and efficiency, and a more robust and resilient system that can withstand unexpected failures.

What is the CAP theorem and how does it apply to cloud software architecture?

The CAP theorem, also known as Brewer's theorem, is a fundamental concept in distributed systems design and stands for Consistency, Availability and Partition Tolerance. It states that in the presence of a network partition, one has to choose between consistency and availability. It's important to note that partition tolerance is not optional in most real-world systems.

1. Consistency: A read operation will always provide the most recent

write. All nodes see the same data at the same time.

2. Availability: A non-failing node will return a valid response to any request, without the guarantee that it contains the most recent write.

3. Partition tolerance: The system continues to function despite arbitrary message loss or failure of part of the system.

Let's define these terms a bit more:

- Consistency: A system is said to be consistent if a transaction starts with the system in a consistent state, and any transaction will take the system from one consistent state to another.

- Availability: A system is said to be available if it remains operational 100% of the time. Although the system might not always be performing at an optimal level, it should appear to the users that it is operational.

- Partition tolerance: A system is said to be partition tolerant if it can sustain any amount of network failure that doesn't result in a failure of the entire network.

The CAP theorem states that a distributed system cannot satisfy all three of these conditions simultaneously; only two out of three can be achieved. Meaning, the three principle guarantees cannot be fulfilled at once. If the network is partitioned due to a network failure between nodes, then one must choose between consistency and availability.

For example, consider a distributed data store that can be deployed across multiple AWS EC2 instances. In case of a network partition, it can either:

- Stay consistent by refusing to serve any requests until the partition resolves (C and P and not A), or

- Stay available by serving requests but with possible stale data, hence compromising consistency (A and P and not C).

This theorem has significant implications on how we build and architect distributed systems. It is used to understand the trade-offs between consistency, availability, and partition tolerance when designing systems that span multiple nodes, servers, or even regions.

In conclusion, the CAP theorem is crucial for designing systems in a distributed computing environment and plays a guiding role in the architecture of cloud services. Although the CAP theorem poses a significant challenge to designers of distributed systems, it also enables them to understand the bounds within which they are operating and guides them in making informed decisions based on the specific requirements and constraints of their applications.

How do you balance costs, performance, and security in a cloud-based system?

Balancing costs, performance, and security in a cloud-based system is a complex process that depends on a variety of factors including the nature of your workload, the sensitivity of your data, and your operational budget. Let's break this down into each component.

1. **Cost**: Cost optimization in the cloud is about using the right types of resources for your workloads and eliminating unneeded resources. AWS offers a number of options that can help reduce costs, such as reserved instances, spot instances, and savings plan.

- **Reserved instances** are instances which are reserved for 1 or 3 year term and provide a significant discount compared to On-Demand pricing.

- **Spot instances** allow you to use spare EC2 computing capacity at a discount of up to 90% compared to On-Demand pricing.

- **Savings plan** provides a cost-effective way to use AWS compute services.

To minimize costs, one can use tools like AWS Cost Explorer or AWS Budgets to closely monitor and manage expenses.

2. **Performance**: Performance optimization in the cloud involves

a mix of optimizing your applications, choosing the right types / sizes of instances, and improving data transfer rates. With the variety of AWS service offerings, it's key to select the suitable services that fit your needs to not compromise on performance.

For example, if your application is CPU-intensive, it would be better to use compute-optimized instances (e.g., C5 instances). If it is memory-intensive, using memory-optimized instances (e.g., R5 instances) would be ideal.

3. **Security**: Security in the cloud is about protecting information and systems. This includes keeping software and configurations up to date, controlling access to your resources, and protecting sensitive data. AWS offers many tools and best practices for maintaining security, such as managing access control through IAM, protecting data in transit and at rest, and monitoring and auditing your resources through AWS CloudTrail and AWS Config.

Balancing these three concerns is a process of making trade-offs based on your specific needs. One way to approach this is by following the AWS Well-Architected Framework, which provides a set of high-level questions you can use to evaluate your architecture. These questions cover five pillars: Operational Excellence, Security, Reliability, Performance Efficiency, and Cost Optimization.

It's often necessary to make some trade-offs between these three areas. For example, increasing performance may lead to higher costs, and improving security might affect performance. However, it's essential to maintain a minimum standard for each area to ensure a healthy and effective cloud architecture.

To give an example, consider the following graph, which depicts a common trade-off scenario:

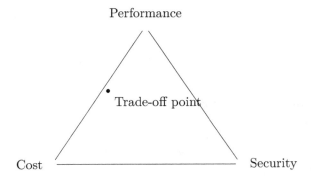

This is a simplified view, but it helps to illustrate how changing one factor can impact the others. To find the right balance, you'll need to carefully evaluate your specific needs and constraints, and adjust your use of AWS resources accordingly.

Remember that balance is a dynamic process, not a one-time setup. Regular monitoring and adjustment should be an integral part of your cloud strategy to ensure optimum cost, performance, and security.

Finally, for complex calculations and deep analysis, you can use AWS's own calculator to provide a detailed set of cost and usage predictions. This tool will help you understand the cost implications of your architectural decisions in more detail.

What does 'Multi-Availability Zone' mean and why is it important?

Multi-Availability Zones (Multi-AZ) is a high-availability feature provided by Amazon Web Services (AWS) and other cloud services to ensure the undisturbed continuity and reliability of applications and services.

In AWS, a region is divided into multiple isolated geographic areas, called Availability Zones (AZs). Each AZ represents a physical data center in the geographical location, containing redundant power supply, networking, and cooling for backup. These AZs are interconnected with high-bandwidth, low-latency networking, over fully redundant, dedicated metro-area fiber providing high-throughput, low-latency networking between AZs.

The purpose of Multi-AZ is to protect the applications from the failure of a single location. Applications can weave together services and resources across several AZs to tolerate infrastructure or system failures, thereby ensuring system availability. For instance, you could configure a primary database in one AZ, and the secondary replica in another AZ. In the case of an AZ failure, the secondary replica automatically becomes the primary, preventing system downtime.

Multi-AZ deployments are an essential part of cloud service design strategy due to:

- **High Availability**: The use of more than one AZ provides the ability to remain operational even if one or more AZs have failed.

- **Fault tolerance**: Multi-AZ architecture can retain data integrity and recover gracefully in the face of partial system failures.

- **Scalability**: Multi-AZ deployments allow distributing instances and directing traffic to different AZs, handling more requests and peak loads.

- **Data Durability**: It helps prevent data loss due to an AZ's disruption by storing backups in another AZ.

What is meant by cloud-native architecture?

Cloud-native architecture is a design approach for building applications that can fully exploit the benefits of cloud computing models like public, private, and hybrid cloud. There are certain principles and practices that are associated with the development and management of these applications.

Cloud-native applications are designed to be platform-independent so they can be deployed in various cloud environments without much modification. They're typically built as a set of small, independent and loosely coupled services, known as microservices, which supports modularity and scalability.

Moreover, these apps are usually containerized, which means each microservice and its dependencies are packaged together as a unit. This not only ensures consistency across various environments but also enables isolation.

Lastly, these applications are built with technologies that support automation and orchestration. This includes continuous integration and delivery (CI/CD), which allows automatic testing and deployment of updates. The architecture also supports automation of operational tasks, like scaling.

The following principles are fundamental to cloud-native architecture:

1. **Microservices Architecture**: Applications are broken down into smaller, manageable, and loosely coupled services which enables agility and scalability. Each microservice can be deployed, upgraded, scaled, and restarted independently of other services in the app.

2. **Containerization**: Each microservice and its dependencies are encapsulated into a container which ensures consistency across multiple environments. Containers are lightweight and can start quickly, making it ideal for a cloud-native application.

3. **Orchestration**: With the help of orchestration tools like Kubernetes, automatic management of containerized applications can be done which includes scheduling, scaling, failover, and deployment.

4. **API-based communication**: Microservices communicate with each other through APIs which reduces the complexity of interaction between microservices and makes them loosely coupled.

5. **Continuous Integration and Continuous Deployment (CI/CD)**: The development process is streamlined with CI/CD

where code changes are frequently integrated, tested, and deployed automatically.

6. **DevOps Practices**: There's a strong culture of collaboration between developers and operations staff with shared responsibility for maintaining the stability and performance of the applications.

7. **Immutable Infrastructure**: Infrastructure is replaced rather than updated on every deployment which leads to consistent and stable environments.

Cloud-native architectures offer numerous benefits like increased agility, resilience, scalability, and speed of deployment, to name a few. However, transition to this architecture requires a shift in organizational culture and development practices, and hence requires careful planning and execution.

1.3   Overview of AWS Cloud Architecture

What are the core components of AWS infrastructure?

The core components of the services provided by AWS Cloud Infrastructure include:

1. Amazon Elastic Compute Cloud (EC2): Amazon EC2 is a web service that provides secure, resizable compute capacity in the cloud. With Amazon EC2, you can rent virtual computers on which to run your own computer applications.

2. Amazon Simple Storage Service (S3): Amazon S3 offers object storage built to store and retrieve any amount of data from anywhere. Users can use it to store backup for disaster recovery, archive, or data analysis.

3. Amazon Relational Database Service (RDS): Amazon RDS makes

it easy to set up, operate, and scale relational databases in the cloud. It provides cost-efficient and resizable capacity whilst automating time-consuming administration tasks such as hardware provisioning, database setup, patching, and backups.

4. AWS Identity and Access Management (IAM): AWS IAM enables you to manage access to AWS services and resources securely. Using AWS IAM, you can create and manage AWS users and groups and use permissions to allow and deny their access to AWS resources.

5. Amazon Virtual Private Cloud (VPC): Amazon VPC lets you provision a logically isolated section of the AWS Cloud where you can launch AWS resources in a virtual network that you define.

6. Elastic Block Store (EBS): Amazon EBS provides persistent block storage volumes for use with Amazon EC2 instances in the AWS Cloud.

7. Elastic Load Balancer (ELB): Amazon ELB automatically distributes incoming application traffic across multiple targets, such as Amazon EC2 instances.

These services enable users to leverage different features for developing a highly robust, scalable, and reliable infrastructure on AWS.

These components integrate with each other to form the AWS Cloud Architecture. The connectivity between these services is demonstrated through the following services interaction graph:

Each arrow in the above graph indicates that the service at the tail can interact with the service at the head. For instance, you can use EC2 instances to store data on S3 or read from it. Similarly, RDS databases can be accessed from EC2 instances and so on.

In real-world use cases, the user may not use all of these services;

their selection depends on the application's requirements and its architecture.

How do Regions, Availability Zones, and Edge Locations work in AWS?

AWS Global Infrastructure is composed of physical locations around the world referred to as Regions, Availability Zones, and Edge Locations.

1. **Regions:** An AWS Region is a physical geographic area of the world where AWS has multiple Availability Zones. Each AWS Region consists of multiple, isolated, and physically separate Data Centers within a geographic area. For example, the US-West-1 region refers to the North California region.

2. **Availability Zones (AZs):** Each Region contains multiple distinct locations called Availability Zones. Each Availability Zone is a fully isolated partition of the AWS global infrastructure. They are physically separated from each other within a region and are interconnected with high-speed private fiber-optic networks. The telecom utility power in each Availability Zone is drawn from different grids for redundancy.

3. **Edge Locations:** Edge Locations are sites deployed in major cities and highly populated areas across the globe. They are used by AWS services like AWS CloudFront and Amazon Route 53 to cache data for low latency delivery (Content Delivery Network) to the end-user. Edge Locations are not necessarily located within a region.

The basic work principle of Regions, Availability Zones, and Edge Locations is as follows:

- When a user uses AWS services, they can select a region to host their services. The choice of a region might depend on factors like latency, compliance requirements, or proximity to customers.

- Within each region, users can leverage different availability zones (AZs) for constructing a highly available and fault-tolerant architecture. For instance, deploying an application across multiple AZs protects against failures within a single AZ.

- AWS services, such as Amazon CloudFront, use globally spread Edge Locations to cache and deliver content closer and faster to customers.

This architecture provides many benefits, including lower latency, higher fault-tolerance, more security, and better compliance capabilities.

Can you describe a typical three-tier architecture in AWS?

A typical three-tier architecture in Amazon Web Services (AWS) includes a Web Tier (also known as Presentation Tier), an Application Tier (or Logic Tier), and a Database Tier (or Data Tier). This model separates the entire system into three subsystems or layers, each handling a specific task, which helps in system management, flexibility, scalability, and security.

Below is the complete description of the three-tier architecture setup in AWS:

Web Tier (Presentation Tier)

This is the topmost layer of the three-tier architecture. In AWS, resources like Amazon EC2 (Elastic Compute Cloud) and Elastic Load Balancing (ELB) serve the web tier's purpose. For example, EC2 instances can host a web application that users interact with directly. At the same time, AWS ELB distributes the incoming app traffic across multiple EC2 instances, across multiple availability zones for high availability and fault tolerance.

Application Tier (Logic Tier)

The Application Tier, also known as the business tier or logic tier, contains the business logic processed by your application, acting as a bridge between the Web and Database Tier. The AWS services typically used for this layer are again EC2 and AWS Lambda. Examples of business logic could include algorithms, rules processing, calculations, etc., as per the requirement of the application.

Database Tier (Data Tier)

This is the lowest or bottom layer in this model, where real data is stored and managed using Database Services. In AWS, services like Amazon RDS (Relational Database System), DynamoDB (NoSQL database service), RedShift (Data Warehousing Solution), etc., are commonly used for this purpose.

This three-tier model helps build highly scalable, maintainable, and secure applications. With AWS, you can scale each tier independently based on your needs. Also, you can apply security at each tier, thus making your system even more secure.

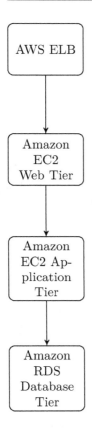

In this example, the arrows signify traffic or commands flowing from one tier to another.

How do you design for high availability and fault tolerance in AWS?

Designing for high availability and fault tolerance in AWS involves several strategies including:

1. Multi-AZ Deployments

2. Auto Scaling

3. Elastic Load Balancing

4. Using Amazon RDS

5. Using Amazon S3

Multi-AZ Deployments

Amazon Web Services provides the ability to deploy your applications in different Availability Zones within a region for high availability and fault tolerance. For example, you have an application that is composed of a front-end web server and a back-end database.

A good example is an AWS EC2 instance. If your instance is terminated or fails, AWS can automatically launch another instance in another availability zone to maintain the availability of your application.

$$\text{availability} = 1 - (1 \text{ - single instance availability})^{N}$$

where N is number of instances.

Auto Scaling

AWS Auto Scaling can help to maintain the availability of your application and limit the impact of component failure by replacing the failed instances.

Elastic Load Balancing

Elastic Load Balancing (ELB) automatically distributes incoming application traffic across multiple Amazon EC2 instances to maintain the availability of your application.

Using Amazon RDS

Amazon RDS (Relational Database Service) can automatically replace the compute capacity in case of a hardware failure with Multi-

AZ deployments.

Using Amazon S3

Amazon S3 is designed for 99.999999999% (11 9's) of durability because it automatically creates and stores copies of all S3 objects across multiple systems.

These strategies can help ensure that your AWS resources remain available and users can reach them in the event of a failure. Implementing high availability, fault tolerance, and recovery should be considered essential and integral parts of any application lifecycle.

Can you explain how the AWS Shared Responsibility Model works?

The AWS Shared Responsibility Model is a framework designed to clearly define the security and compliance-related roles and responsibilities of both AWS (Amazon Web Services) and the customer (or AWS user). This model promotes better security and system integrity by ensuring that each party knows what they are responsible for.

The model can be broken down into two broad components:

1. **Security "of" the cloud**: This is AWS's responsibility and involves protecting the infrastructure that runs all of the services in the AWS Cloud. This typically includes hardware, software, networking, and facilities that AWS provides to run its services.

Areas involved typically include:

- Infrastructure (global compute, storage, database, and networking capabilities)

- Hardware, software, and network infrastructure

- Managed services (databases, machine learning, analytics, queuing, searching, emailing, notifications, and others)

2. **Security "in" the cloud**: This is the customer's responsibility and depends on the AWS services that a customer selects. The user is responsible for managing the guest operating system (including updates and security patches), other associated application software as well as the configuration of the AWS provided security group firewall.

Areas involved typically include:

- Customer data

- Platform, applications, identity & access management

- Operating system, network & firewall configuration

- Client & end-point protection

- Encryption & network traffic protection

Looking at the AWS Shared Responsibility Model, one can imagine something like the following:

Responsibility	Owner
AWS Global Infrastructure	AWS
Managed Services	AWS
Customer Data	Customer
Applications	Customer
OS, Network & Firewall Configuration	Customer
Client & End-point Protection	Customer
Encryption & Network Traffic Protection	Customer

In conclusion, it's important to understand that security and compliance is a shared responsibility between AWS and the customer. This shared model can help relieve the customer's operational burden as AWS operates, manages and controls the components from the host operating system and virtualization layer down to the physical security of the facilities in which the service operates.

How does AWS manage data replication and redundancy?

AWS manages data replication and redundancy through an extensive, sophisticated set of mechanisms, which rely heavily on their internal networks and services.

There are two primary ways AWS achieves redundancy:

1. **Data Replication**: AWS routinely replicates stored data across multiple servers to ensure availability in case of failure. This makes the system resilient to problems that affect individual servers or entire data centers.

2. **Geographic Redundancy**: AWS may store copies of data in different geographical locations to safeguard against location-specific issues, such as natural disasters or network outages.

Data Replication

To manage data replication, AWS uses services like Simple Storage Service (S3), DynamoDB, and Elastic Block Store (EBS), each of which provides different ways to handle replication.

* **Amazon S3**: S3 offers a feature called cross-region replication (CRR). Once CRR is enabled for a bucket, all objects uploaded to the bucket are automatically replicated to a destination bucket, which can be in a different region.

* **Amazon DynamoDB**: DynamoDB supports global tables, which automatically replicate tables across multiple AWS regions.

* **Amazon EBS**: EBS snapshots can be copied and recreated in other regions.

Redundancy

When we talk about AWS redundancy, some important services include Amazon S3, Amazon Glacier, and Amazon Elastic File System

(EFS).

* **Amazon S3**: S3 redundantly stores data in multiple facilities and on multiple devices within a facility. It leverages a concept called "Bucket" which is a container for data, and the data stored in it (in the form of objects) can be protected by versioning, allowing for the restoration of objects to a previous state.

* **Amazon Glacier**: This service is designed to provide average annual durability of 99.999999999% (11 9s) for an archive. It achieves this high level of redundancy by persistently storing your data across multiple Availability Zones in multiple Devices.

* **Amazon EFS**: EFS automatically and transparently replicates your file system data and metadata within and across multiple Availability Zones.

In summary, replication and redundancy in AWS is achieved through the use of various AWS storage services, and it's automatically baked into their offerings. This ensures data durability and availability, protecting against both component failure and major incidents.

What is Amazon VPC and why is it important?

Amazon Virtual Private Cloud (Amazon VPC) is a service that lets you launch Amazon Web Services (AWS) resources in a logically isolated virtual network that you define. Users have full control over the virtual networking environment, including selection of your own IP address range, creation of subnets, and configuration of route tables and network gateways.

This logically isolated space is important for several reasons:

1. **Security:** With Amazon VPC, you can use multiple layers of security, including security groups and network access control lists to help control access to Amazon EC2 instances in each subnet. This allows security to be as restrictive or permissive as needed, down to

the individual instance level.

2. **Design Customized Network Architecture:** Amazon VPC provides you with the flexibility to design your network configurations
as closely as possible to your actual network requirement or architecture. You can create a public-facing subnet for your webservers that
have access to the internet, and place your backend systems such as
databases or application servers in a private-facing subnet with no
internet access.

3. **Direct Connectivity to Your Corporate Datacenter:** Amazon
VPC allows for the provision of a Hardware Virtual Private Network
(VPN) connection between your corporate datacenter and your VPC,
to leverage the AWS cloud as an extension of your corporate datacenter.

4. **Advanced Networking Features:** Amazon VPC provides networking features such as network address translation (NAT), access
control list (ACL), routing tables, private and public subnets, VPNs,
and more.

Simplified Diagram of an Amazon VPC:

Amazon VPC

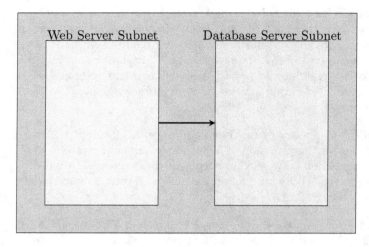

In this diagram, the web server subnet is exposed to the internet for handling web traffic while the database server subnet is isolated within the VPC for security, demonstrating the customizable nature of VPC configurations.

How do you choose the right AWS services for a particular use case?

Choosing the right AWS services for a particular use case depends on several factors such as the nature of the application, the expected workload, security compliance requirements, budget constraints, and others. Here's a general approach to choosing the right AWS services:

1. **Requirements Analysis**: First, you need to understand the requirements of your application. This includes understanding the workload patterns (predictable/unpredictable), necessary compliance/security measures, data storage requirements, processing capability needs, and amounts of data transfer expected.

2. **Service Selection**: Based on these requirements, you can choose the right AWS services. Here are some typical services for different requirements:

- Compute: Services such as EC2 (Elastic Compute Cloud), ECS (Elastic Container Service), AWS Lambda for Function-as-a-Service architecture, Batch for batch computing, or Lightsail for deploying lightweight applications.

- Storage: S3 (Simple Storage Service) for object storage, EFS (Elastic File System) for NFS file systems, or Glacier for archive data.

- Databases: Services like RDS (Relational Database Service) for relational databases, DynamoDB for NoSQL, Redshift for Data warehousing, and ElastiCache for in-memory caching.

- Networking: Services such as VPC (Virtual Private Cloud) for secure and customizable virtual networks, Route 53 for DNS, API Gateway for API development, and Direct Connect for establishing dedicated connections to AWS.

These are just examples, and AWS offers several other services as well.

3. **Trade-Offs & Optimization**: This is the trickiest part. You often need to trade-off between cost, performance, complexity, etc. You want to optimize the use of resources while meeting your business/application requirements. AWS Cost Explorer, AWS Trusted Advisor and various AWS calculators can help you in making these decisions.

4. **Testing**: Finally, testing the selected services with your application's workflows is necessary. You can monitor the performance, cost, and other critical aspects using services like AWS CloudWatch and tweak your decisions as necessary.

Remember, there's no overall "best" service – the right one depends on your application's specific needs. AWS architecture is designed to be highly flexible and versatile, allowing you to choose a tailored solution that suits your use-case the best. Thus, understanding your application's requirements and AWS services is key to deploying robust, cost-effective, and efficient systems in the cloud.

For example, let's consider a use-case of a mobile gaming application that requires quick response times and a scalable database for storing high scores globally. You will need to use AWS Lambda for processing, Amazon DynamoDB for NoSQL database service and AWS Cognito for user sign-up and sign-in, etc.

On the other hand, if you are storing large amounts of infrequently accessed data such as logs from your web server, you might use Amazon S3 for storage, Amazon Glacier for archival and AWS Athena service to query your logs.

These examples illustrate how different use-cases require different combinations of services. The art of AWS Cloud Architecture lies in mixing and matching these services to create the optimum architecture for your application.

Can you discuss how security is handled in AWS?

Security in Amazon Web Services (AWS) is tackled in a comprehensive, end-to-end strategy. It relies on different types of controls to maintain the overall security health. AWS offers multiple layers of security, including secure computation, storage, database services, networking, and mobile devices, among others.

Among the crucial aspects of AWS cloud security are:

- **Identity and Access Management (IAM):** This service allows the management of users and their access to AWS resources. An administrator can create and assign different roles and permissions to individual users, groups or services, defining who can take action on particular resources.

- **Detective Controls:** AWS CloudTrail, AWS CloudWatch, and AWS Config are among the tools that AWS offers for logging and monitoring the environment and actions taken within it.

- **Infrastructure Protection:** AWS has several services for network security such as Amazon Virtual Private Cloud (VPC), AWS Shield (a managed Distributed Denial of Service protection service), as well as AWS WAF (a web application firewall).

- **Data Protection:** AWS provides features such as encryption for stored or in-transit data and the ability to manage keys using AWS Key Management Service.

- **Incident Response:** AWS provides services such as Amazon GuardDuty (threat detection service), AWS CloudTrail (logs of API activity), and AWS Config (records of changes to resources in your environment) for response and remediation actions when a potential incident occurs.

Below is a representation of the AWS Cloud Security:

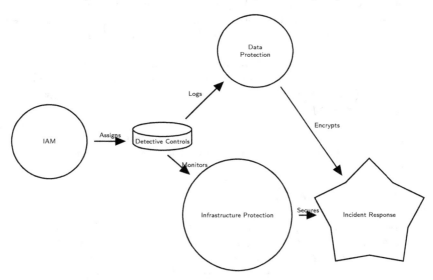

This image illustrates the relationship between the different components of AWS security. IAM assigns permissions, detective controls log and monitor activities, Infrastructure protection secures the network, data protection secures the data, and incident response handles potential incidents.

AWS follows a shared responsibility model for security. AWS is responsible for securing the underlying infrastructure, while users are responsible for securing anything they put on the cloud or connect to the cloud such as data, applications, and operating systems.

Always remember that the security model is adaptable, enabling you to pick the suitable service or services based on your specific needs and circumstances.

How does AWS support scaling and elasticity?

Amazon Web Services (AWS) is a highly scalable and elastic cloud computing platform that uses distributed IT infrastructure. The key concepts of scaling on AWS are elasticity and scalability.

Scalability refers to your application's ability to add or remove resources to meet your current requirements, either by means of vertical scaling (increasing the computational power of individual resources) or horizontal scaling (increasing the number of resources).

Elasticity, on the other hand, is a cloud computing property that enables systems to automatically provision and deprovision resources to meet workload demands.

Auto Scaling

AWS Auto Scaling monitors your applications and automatically adjusts capacity to meet demand. It can be utilized to scale for multiple services, ensuring that your application always has the right amount of capacity to manage its workload. AWS Auto Scaling employs scaling plans to manage the scalable resources that support your application.

Elastic Load Balancing

Elastic Load Balancing (ELB) automatically distributes incoming application traffic across multiple targets, including EC2 instances, containers, and IP addresses, which increases the availability of your application.

The services ELB offers include Application Load Balancer that operates at the request level (layer 7), Network Load Balancer operating at the transport level (layer 4), and Classic Load Balancer, which operates at both the request and transport level.

Elasticity via EC2

EC2 instances provide an auto-scaling feature which uses CloudWatch to set conditions for scaling up (creating new instances) and scaling down (terminating instances). This can happen automatically based on predefined rules such as CPU utilization crossing a threshold level.

Using EC2, a scale-out action could be triggered when the average CPU usage of some instances crosses a designated threshold (e.g., 70%) over a period of 5 minutes. Conversely, a scale-in action could be triggered when CPU usage drops under another threshold level (for example 30%).

Such powerful features facilitate application high availability and fault tolerance, thus supporting high user populations and workload fluctuation.

In conclusion, AWS provides various tools for achieving both scaling and elasticity. AWS handles the complex, error-prone, and time-consuming processes of provisioning and managing infrastructure resources in real-time to meet your business needs.

Chapter 2

Software Architecture Principles

This chapter demystifies the core principles underpinning software architecture, an essential discipline that lays the groundwork for effective and efficient software systems. At the heart of this exploration is a deep dive into various architectural styles and patterns, where readers will discover the nuances between different design structures and their implications for diverse applications. The narrative then shifts to the revered SOLID principles, shedding light on foundational design methodologies that foster robust and adaptable software creations. Equipped with these foundational insights, the chapter delves into the art and science of crafting high-level design documents and diagrams. These tools are instrumental in visually representing architectural decisions and ensuring alignment across diverse project stakeholders.

Subsequently, the chapter tackles the often daunting task of making technology stack decisions, equipping readers with strategies to choose the right tools for their unique project requirements. Rounding off the chapter is a deep dive into the essential attributes of any successful software system: scalability, reliability, security, and maintainability. By encapsulating these principles, this chapter provides an invaluable blueprint for aspiring architects and seasoned professionals alike, illuminating the methodologies that propel successful software endeavors.

2.1   Architectural Styles and Patterns

What is the difference between architectural styles and architectural patterns?

In the field of Software Architecture, the terms "architectural styles" and "architectural patterns" are used interchangeably by some, however they represent two different concepts.

Architectural Styles: An architectural style, also known as architectural pattern, is a set of principles—a coarse grained pattern that provides an abstract framework for a family of systems. An architectural style improves partitioning and promotes design reuse by providing solutions to frequently recurring problems. You can think of architecture styles and patterns as sets of principles that shape an application.

Put another way, an architectural style is a specific method of construction, characterized by the features that make it notable. A style may include such elements as form, method of construction, materials, and regional character. In terms of software architecture, it may refer to specific structural aspects such as microservices architecture, service-oriented architecture, monolithic architecture, etc.

Architectural Patterns: An architectural pattern is a general, reusable solution to a commonly occurring problem in software architecture within a given context. Architectural patterns are similar to software design pattern but have a broader scope.

Architectural patterns have an extensive impact on the code base, most often impacting multiple components across multiple systems. They provide the means to solve common architectural problems like handling user requests, integrating disparate systems, and setting up databases.

For example, Model-View-Controller (MVC) is a widely used architectural pattern for creating user interfaces where the application data (Model), user interface (View), and input control (Controller) are separated from each other.

In conclusion, an architectural style is a high-level category, and a specific architectural pattern essentially represents a particular implementation strategy within a given style.

This distinction can be illustrated as follows:

Architectural Styles	Architectural Patterns
Event-driven architecture	Publisher-subscriber
Layered architecture	N-tier, Client-server
Interpreted systems	Rule-based systems
Microservices	Broker topology, Chain of responsibility

This table, although not exhaustive, shows some common examples of architectural styles and corresponding patterns. Each "style" represents a broad way of structuring software, while each "pattern" is a more specific approach that can fit into one or more styles.

Can you explain the Model-View-Controller (MVC) pattern?

The View-Controller (MVC) pattern is a software design pattern commonly used for developing user interfaces that divides the related program logic into three interconnected elements: the Model, the View, and the Controller. Here is how they work:

1. **Model:** This is the central component of the pattern, and it's directly managing the data, logic, and rules of the application. A model can be understood as a data structure. For example, a Customer object will retrieve the customer information from the database, manipulate it, and update it data back to the database or use it to render data.

2. **View:** A view is an output representation of the information, such as a chart, diagram, or table. Multiple views of the same information are possible. For example, the customer information could be displayed as a bar chart for a CFO and as a data table for a salesperson.

3. **Controller:** The controller accepts input and converts it to commands for the model or view. For instance, the controller can call methods in the model to update a customer record (a process known as updating data in the database) or retrieve the customer record and then return the updated version to the view to display the updated information (a process known as reading data from the database).

In terms of an MVC diagram, you can visualize the pattern's structure as:

Controller

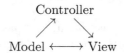

Model ⟷ View

The arrows represent the flow of data and control:

- The controller receives an input.

- The controller then processes the input via commands to the model.

- The model retrieves or adjusts information, then sends that information to the View.

- The view presents the output to the user.

The main advantage of MVC architecture is the decoupling of these three components. This improves code organization, allows for efficient code reuse, and can significantly reduce the complexity of the application architecture. Furthermore, this approach makes it easier to modify or extend your application over time, since changes to one component (e.g., changing how data is displayed in the View) should not affect the other two components.

How would you choose an appropriate architectural pattern for a particular application?

When considering the choice of an architectural pattern for any application, there are numerous factors to consider. Here are some of those key factors:

1. **Functional Requirements**: It refers to the operations that the system should be able to perform. Understanding functional requirements helps to identify the complexity of the system, thereby helping to determine the right architectural pattern.

2. **Non-Functional Requirements**: These are the requirements related to system performance, security, usability, compatibility. Depending upon what non-functional requirements are more critical, the architecture pattern can be decided.

3. **Business Domain**: The domain in which your application belongs can influence the selection of a suitable architectural pattern. For example, an enterprise business application might benefit from a layered architecture, while a cloud-native application might benefit from a microservices architecture.

4. **Scalability**: If your application needs to handle large loads or scale dynamically based on load, an architecture style that supports horizontal scaling, like microservices, is preferable.

5. **Development Time and Cost**: Some architectural patterns may be more complex and require more time to implement, which will increase the development cost.

Choosing an appropriate architectural pattern involves analyzing all these factors and more. Here are a few basic pattern options and where they might be most suitable:

* **Layered architecture**: Best suited for simple, traditional web applications. For example, a monolithic application can use a three-layered approach with the presentation, business logic, and data layers.

* **Event-Driven architecture**: Suitable for applications likely to handle massive to moderate streams of data. IoT applications, analytics platforms are common applications of this approach.

* **Microservices architecture**: Best for complex systems needing high scalability and high-speed iteration.

Assuming you have an online e-commerce project which needs to be scalable and fault-tolerant with a quick iteration time, you could choose the Microservices Architectural pattern. In such an architecture, each component of the e-commerce system (like user management, product catalog, orders, payments) will be a separate service, which leads to easy scalability as per load on a particular component. It also ensures fault isolation.

The following decision tree is an example of how to choose a pattern, bearing in mind this is a simplified approach:

```
if (Performance Critical)
   if (Modulary independence)
      'Use Microservices'
   else if (Complexity is Not High)
      'Use Layered Architecture or MVC based on the requirments'
   else
      'Use Event Driven Architecture'
else if (Security Critical)
   'Use a Service-Oriented Architecture'
else
   Use Monolithic Architecture
```

Remember, no single architecture pattern is a silver bullet and the best architecture often is a combination of multiple patterns. It's also crucial to consider the principles of "The Twelve-Factor App" (https://12factor.net/) when designing and developing a modern scalable application. These are particularly helpful in designing cloud-native, scalable, and maintainable applications.

Lastly, AWS provides many well-architected white papers and frameworks (https://aws.amazon.com/architecture/) that can provide guidance on best practices for building applications on AWS. They can be of great help while deciding the architecture pattern.

Can you discuss some pros and cons of the microservices architecture style?

Microservices is an architectural style that structures an application as a collection of loosely coupled services. This architectural method is considered ideal when you need to create applications that need to scale and evolve rapidly. Services in a microservices architecture are often processes that communicate over a network to fulfill a particular goal.

Below are some pros and cons of microservices architectural style.

Pros:

1. **Independent Deployment**: Small, focused services can be updated, deployed and scaled independently.

2. **Fault Isolation**: A process failure should not bring the whole system down. Hardware issues should affect just that service.

3. **Mixed Technology Stacks**: Services can be written in different programming languages and use different data storage technologies.

4. **Granular Scaling**: Services that require more resources can be scaled independently.

5. **Optimized for The Cloud**: Microservices take full advantage of cloud platforms, particularly around continuous integration and continuous deployment.

Cons:

1. **Service Coordination**: Larger numbers of services can lead to difficulty in coordinating tasks and transactions that span multiple services.

2. **Data Duplication**: Every services maintain their own domain data to achieve decoupled architecture. This can lead to data duplication.

3. **Network Latency**: Communication between services is often done over a network which is slower than in-process calls, leading to increased latency.

4. **Testing**: Writing test scripts can be difficult because each service is a separate component.

5. **Cultural, Organisational Shift**: Microservices require the whole organization to shift their thinking to deliver software in a new way.

What is a layered architectural style and where is it most effectively used?

A layered architectural style is one of the common architecture patterns used in software development. It entirely separates concerns among components of the software, making a system well-organized, easy to maintain, and scalable.

A layered architecture is organised in hierarchical layers where each layer performs specific operations. The most typical number of layers in a layered architecture is four. These generally comprise the Presentation Layer (User Interface), Application Layer (Business Logic), Business Layer (Business Rules), and Data Access Layer (Data Persistence).

Presentation Layer
Application Layer
Business Layer
Data Access Layer

Layers in a layered architecture communicate in a bi-directional manner, meaning each layer can exchange information with the layer directly above or below it. However, a more restrictive rule, as in the case of a strict layered architecture, is that a layer can only communicate with the layer below it.

This architecture style is most effectively used in applications that need clear separation of concerns, those that require a high level of maintainability, and in applications that can afford considerable overhead in the communication between layers. For instance, enterprise applications, where business rules often change, greatly benefit from the adaptable nature of this architectural style. The layered architecture also proves useful in real life cloud services. AWS itself is built as a layered system, allowing devs to utilise services across the AWS stack without needing to be concerned with lower-level operational details.

However, one downside to the layered architecture style is the potential performance overhead, especially in scenarios with large numbers of requests. The request must go through several layers until it gets to the correct one, which can take considerable time. In these cases, other architecture styles like Microservices might be more appropriate.

How can the publish-subscribe pattern be used in system design?

The publish-subscribe (pub/sub) pattern is a software architectural pattern widely used in distributed systems where senders of messages, known as publishers, do not program the messages to be sent directly to specific receivers, known as subscribers. Instead, published messages are categorized into classes without knowledge of which subscribers, if any, there may be. Similarly, subscribers express interest in one or more classes and only receive messages that are of interest, without knowledge of which publishers, if any, there are.

This decoupling of publishers and subscribers can allow for greater scalability and a more dynamic network topology. For example, in a cloud environment like AWS, you could have an S3 bucket where data files are dropped (publisher), and a Lambda function that triggers upon the drop event to process these files (subscriber). The S3 bucket does not need to know about the Lambda function, and the Lambda function does not depend directly on the S3 bucket. They are decoupled, yet the system works in harmony thanks to the pub/sub model.

Mathematically speaking, imagine a system where there are 'n' publishers and 'm' subscribers. In a traditional direct point-to-point communication setup (request-response model), each publisher would need to send its message to each subscriber individually. The complexity of this operation grows linearly with the number of subscribers, rendering this approach as 'O(nm)'.

However, in a pub/sub model, each publisher just publishes their message (or their "class"), and the message gets sent to all subscribers interested in that class, regardless of their number. Therefore, the complexity of this operation becomes 'O(n) + O(m)', which is a much more scalable approach for large distributed systems.

The graph below illustrates these complexities:

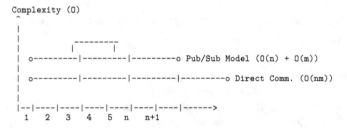

```
Complexity (O)

 |
 |
 |            ---------
 |           |         |
 |  o--------|---------|---------o Pub/Sub Model (O(n) + O(m))
 |
 |  o--------|---------|---------|---------o Direct Comm. (O(nm))
 |
 |
 |--|----|----|----|----|----|----|------>
    1    2    3    4    5    n    n+1
```

In the AWS environment, the pub/sub pattern can be implemented with services like SNS (Simple Notification Service) and SQS (Simple Queue Service). SNS works by pushing messages to all subscribers when a publisher sends a message to a topic, while SQS works by having messages pulled by the subscribers, providing a reliable, highly-scalable hosted queue for storing messages as they travel between different systems.

Pub/Sub systems can provide robustness (a publisher failure won't affect the subscribers & vice-versa), scalability (publishers and subscribers can be added independently of each other), and temporal decoupling (publishers and subscribers do not need to be actively interacting at the time of data transmission).

What are some architectural patterns that are conducive to high scalability?

There are several architectural patterns that are conducive to high scalability. Here are some of the most commonly used in AWS Cloud Software Architecture:

1. **Microservices Architecture**: This architecture divides applications into smaller, loosely coupled services which communicate with each other using APIs. Each microservice runs its own process and communicates through a mechanism, often HTTP/REST with JSON. This style is highly scale-responsive as each service can be scaled independently according to the demand.

2. **Event-Driven Architecture (EDA)**: This design pattern operates upon the occurrence of certain events. In a highly-scalable, event-driven system, services communicate with event notifications. One service executes a function, emits an event while another service listens and subsequently triggers an event. It allows for high level of scaling, as tasks are processed asynchronously and parallel.

3. **Serverless Architecture**: Serverless patterns abstract the server layer entirely and only charge based on resource consumption. Developers don't have to worry about provisioning and managing servers when at peak traffic. A serverless function scales horizontally, not vertically meaning it scales by adding more instances of the function to handle incoming events.

4. **CQRS (Command Query Responsibility Segregation)**: CQRS suggests splitting an application into two parts - command side which is responsible for handling all update requests and query side which

handles data read. This results in a flexible and highly scalable architecture, as read and write workloads can scale independently.

5. **Sharding Patterns**: Sharding involves splitting a database into small, manageable pieces (shards) and distributing them across different machines. This pattern increases the performance and speed of applications as it handles high traffic by spreading the load.

Each of these patterns has its own pros and cons, and the choice of which to use largely depends on specific application requirements and constraints.

Can you give an example of the use of a peer-to-peer (P2P) architectural style?

A classic example of Peer-to-peer (P2P) architectural style is BitTorrent, a protocol supporting the practice of peer-to-peer file sharing that is used to distribute large amounts of data over the internet.

BitTorrent does not rely on a central server for storing files. Instead, it allows users to connect directly to each other to download and upload files. Here is the process:

1. A user, called a "leecher", wants to download a file.

2. They download a small .torrent file from BitTorrent's website, which contains metadata about the file to be downloaded and about the tracker (a server that coordinates the file distribution).

3. The BitTorrent client software reads this file and connects to specified trackers, which keep track of all users who are downloading or have completely downloaded the file.

4. The tracker sends a list of peers to the client, who then directly connects to those peers to request pieces of the file.

5. Once pieces of the file are downloaded, they can also be uploaded to other peers. This is essentially sharing the file among multiple peers, greatly reducing the load on any single server.

This process can be represented as a graph:

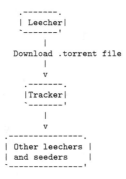

In short, BitTorrent uses a P2P architecture to decentralize file distribution, increase redundancy, and reduce reliance on a single point of failure (i.e., a central server).

However, it is important to know that P2P systems carry vulnerabilities such as an increased risk of data corruption, data piracy, or dissemination of inappropriate or illegal content. For these reasons, P2P systems take advantage of cryptographic protocols to ensure data integrity and secure data transmission.

How can the event-driven architectural style improve system performance?

Event-driven architecture (EDA) can substantially improve system performance in several ways:

1. **Asynchronous Processing**: EDA allows asynchronous processing of events, reducing latency and drastically improving response times in distributed systems. With EDA, an event producer emits an event and continues processing without waiting for the event consumer. This is particularly beneficial in cases where immediate responsiveness is more important than completing a task immediately,

as it allows a system to handle high volumes of inputs in real time while processing them asynchronously - a model which is drastically more scalable than synchronous, step-by-step processing.

2. **Scalability**: EDA provides a high degree of scalability, allowing the system to cope efficiently with increases in workload. As each event is processed individually, additional resources can be allocated dynamically (vertical scaling) or additional instances can be created to handle the events (horizontal scaling).

3. **User Experience**: EDA improves the perceived system performance from the end-user perspective. Take user registration as an example. In traditional request/response architecture, the user signup request might involve verifying the user's email, sending a welcome email, and creating an account record in the database. In the worst case scenario, the user would be waiting for all these tasks to finish. However, using EDA: the user signup generates an event (user registered), a database service listens to that event and creates an account, an email service listens and sends a welcome email. The user can see the account created immediately, improving perceived performance.

4. **Resource Optimization**: EDA optimizes resource utilization by decoupling the event producers from the consumers, reducing the risk of resource congestion and allowing for proper load balancing strategies

Using AWS as an example with the Pub-Sub architectural pattern:

> Services (event publishers) send messages to a topic in Amazon Simple Notification Service (SNS)
>
> Amazon Simple Queue Service (SQS) queues, or AWS Lambda functions (event subscribers) process the messages
>
> Pubs (e.g. e-commerce order service) and subscribers (e.g. email notification service) are decoupled

Here, the AWS services SNS, SQS, and Lambda enable EDA that

improves system performance with optimized architectural patterns.

However, it's important to note that while EDA has clear benefits in improving system performance, it isn't always the best solution. Designing and deploying an event-driven system can be complex because of the need to coordinate multiple distributed, asynchronous components. Moreover, debugging and tracing issues in these systems can be difficult due to their asynchronous and distributed nature. Thus, one should decide the use of EDA based on specific case requirement and feasibility.

Can you describe a real-world application where you used a specific architectural style or pattern?

It's important to first understand that architectural styles and patterns are a strategic choice made during designing a cloud software solution. Different architectural styles and patterns come with their own sets of benefits and trade-offs. Based on specific needs of the application, like scalability, security, ease of deployment, fault tolerance and so on, we identify the right architectural style or pattern.

One real-world application example can be the design and deployment of a large scale, distributed web application using the Microservices Architecture on the Amazon Web Services (AWS) platform.

Microservices Architecture is an architectural pattern where an application is designed as a collection of loosely coupled services. These services are fine-grained, can be developed independently and can be deployed and scaled individually. They interact with each other using APIs over a network.

Consider an ecommerce web application that we had to design for a client. The application includes modules like user management, product catalog, order management and so on. Instead of designing this as a monolithic application, we chose for the microservices architecture.

This application was built and deployed on AWS using various AWS services. For example, each microservice can be a separate Elastic Beanstalk application or can be containerized using Amazon ECS or EKS. Amazon API Gateway is used as the entry point to these microservices. AWS Lambda functions can also be used, especially when you want to fully leverage the benefits of microservices architecture, where services can be independently deployed and scaled.

Using microservices architecture, each module of the ecommerce application can be treated as separate services, which can be independently developed, deployed, and scaled. These services can be built using the best technologies and programming languages suitable for their specific needs.

For instance:

- The user management service can be built using Node.js and backed by an Amazon DynamoDB table.

- The product catalog service may be developed in Java and use Amazon Aurora as the database.

- The order management service can be built using .NET and use Amazon RDS with SQL Server as the database.

This architectural pattern provides benefits like flexibility in technology choices, independent scalability for each service, fault isolation (failure in one service does not impact others), and makes it easier to understand, develop and test.

The following figure shows the architectural diagram of the microservices based ecommerce application on AWS.

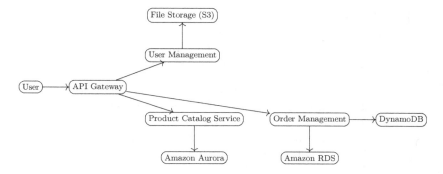

Each rectangle above represents a microservice or AWS service that communicates with other services over the network. The arrows represent the flow of information between services.

This example shows how AWS can enable the deployment of a Microservices Architecture, improving the scalability, resilience, and agility of your applications.

2.2 Design Principles (like SOLID)

Can you explain each of the SOLID principles and why they're important in object-oriented design?

The SOLID principles are a set of design principles that are meant to make software designs more understandable, flexible, and maintainable. These principles were promoted by Robert C. Martin, and they are widely used in modern object-oriented design.

1. **S: Single Responsibility Principle (SRP):** This principle states that a class should have only one reason to change. This means that a class should only have one job. If a class has more than one responsibility, it becomes coupled. A change to one responsibility results in modification of the other responsibility. It's about cohesion: doing one thing well.

For example, consider an application that takes a collection of shapes—circles, and squares—and calculates the area of each. According to the SRP, we would create one class to calculate the area of circles and another to calculate the area of squares.

2. **O: Open/Closed Principle (OCP):** This principle states that classes should be open for extension, but closed for modification. This can be done by using abstract interfaces, where the implementation can be changed and multiple implementations could be created and polymorphically substituted for each other.

A typical example would be a sorting algorithm. We could define an interface 'Sorter' that sorts an array, and we can have multiple implementations like 'QuickSort', 'MergeSort', etc. The sorting routine would be closed for modification but still open for extension as we can add more sorting algorithms.

3. **L: Liskov Substitution Principle (LSP):** Subtypes must be substitutable for their base types without altering the correctness of the program. This principle is just an extension of the substitution principle present in inheritance. If a class is a subtype of another class, then objects of the subtype should be able to replace objects of the original class without affecting program correctness.

For example, if 'Rectangle' is a subclass of 'Polygon', then wherever we're using 'Polygon' objects, we should be able to use 'Rectangle's without causing any issues or changes in behavior.

4. **I: Interface Segregation Principle (ISP):** This principle states that a class should not be forced to implement interfaces it does not use. Instead of one fat interface, multiple small interfaces are preferred based on groups of methods, each one serving one submodule.

For instance, if you have an interface 'Printer' with methods 'print', 'fax', and 'scan', not all printers can fax and scan, so they should not implement fax and scan.

5. **D: Dependency Inversion Principle (DIP):** This principle states that high-level modules should not depend on low-level mod-

ules. Both should depend on abstractions. In addition, abstractions should not depend on details. Details should depend on abstractions.

A classic example of DIP would be lamp (high-level module) not depending on the button (low-level module), but both depending on the switch (an abstraction). The button is a detail and should depend on the abstraction.

Overall, these principles lead to a coupling that is reduced and an application that can be more easily maintained over time. Despite requirements' changes, the system can be easily changed with minimal side effects.

How would you apply the Open/Closed Principle in a real-world application?

The Open/Closed Principle (OCP) is one of the five principles of SOLID, an acronym coined by Robert C. Martin in the early 2000s as a guideline for object-oriented design and programming. The Open/-Closed Principle states that "software entities (classes, modules, functions, etc.) should be open for extension, but closed for modification". This aims to help reduce the risk of introducing new bugs when the business requirements change or additional functionality is needed.

The concept behind OCP is that once a module has been developed and tested, the code should not be modified. Any new behavior should be implemented as new code, not by changing existing code, thus preventing potential new bugs in already working code.

Let's assume a hypothetical scenario where we have an AWS-based application that processes system logs. Consider a 'LogProcessor' class which processes different types of logs:

```
class LogProcessor {
    void process(Log log) {
        if (log instanceof SystemLog) {
            // Processing system logs
        } else if (log instanceof ApplicationLog) {
            // Processing application logs
```

```
    }
      // More log types go here in the future
    }
  }
```

In this architecture, any new type of log would lead us to modify the 'LogProcessor' class, violating the OCP.

A better approach compliant with OCP would imply abstracting 'LogProcessor' and extending it for each log type.

```
interface LogProcessor {
    void process(Log log);
}

class SystemLogProcessor implements LogProcessor {
    void process(Log log) {
        // Processing system logs
    }
}

class ApplicationLogProcessor implements LogProcessor {
    void process(Log log) {
        // Processing application logs
    }
}
```

In the future, to introduce a new log type, we can simply extend our 'LogProcessor' interface without modifying the existing code but by adding new code, adhering to the Open/Closed Principle.

In a real-world application, introducing new functionalities or modifying existing features would often involve code changes. However, these changes should be designed and conducted in a way that doesn't disrupt the existing functionality. Our design should be flexible and open for extensions without necessitating modification in existing modules.

Applying SOLID principles, such as OCP, in AWS cloud software architecture plays a crucial role in ensuring robust, maintainable, and flexible systems. These principles guide us in making systems that respond well to change and are easy to understand, thus aiding both scalability and reliability.

Can you give an example of the Liskov Substitution Principle being violated?

The Liskov Substitution Principle (LSP) is one of the most important concepts in object-oriented programming and is a part of SOLID principles. The LSP was defined by Barbara Liskov in 1987. It states that, if a program is using a Base class, then the reference to the Base class can be replaced with a Derived class without affecting the correctness of the program.

In other words, all objects of a superclass should be able to be replaced with objects of a subclass without causing any issues to the program.

Violations of the Liskov Substitution Principle can introduce bugs and complexities into a codebase. Let's see an example where the LSP is violated.

Consider two classes, 'Rectangle' and 'Square'. In an inheritance hierarchy, you might say that a 'Square' is-a 'Rectangle', and thus create the class 'Square' as a subclass of 'Rectangle'.

```python
class Rectangle:
    def __init__(self, width, height):
        self._height = height
        self._width = width

    def set_width(self, width):
        self._width = width

    def set_height(self, height):
        self._height = height

    def get_area(self):
        return self._width * self._height

class Square(Rectangle):
    def __init__(self, size):
        super().__init__(size, size)

    def set_width(self, width):
        super().set_width(width)
        super().set_height(width)

    def set_height(self, height):
        super().set_width(height)
        super().set_height(height)
```

While it is mathematically logical, this violates the LSP in terms of its behavior.

A 'Rectangle''s width can change independently of its height but, if you use a 'Square' and 'Rectangle' interchangeably (as you should be able to, by the LSP), this can cause unexpected behavior.

```
def print_area(rectangle):
    rectangle.set_width(4)
    rectangle.set_height(5)
    print(rectangle.get_area(), "Expected:␣20")

rectangle = Rectangle(0, 0)
print_area(rectangle)

square = Square(0)
print_area(square)
```

When the 'print_area()' function is passed a 'Square', it will not return the expected result. Hence, this code does not follow LSP. This occurs because the behaviors of the 'Rectangle' and 'Square' classes are not entirely compatible.

When designing and developing classes, care should be taken to ensure that superclass and subclass can be exchanged seamlessly with no changes in expected behavior. Thus, any class which is the child class of a parent class should be substitutable for its superclass.

How can the Dependency Inversion Principle improve the maintainability of a system?

The Dependency Inversion Principle (DIP) is a fundamental principle of Object Oriented Programming (OOP) that plays a crucial role in enabling more maintainable, flexible systems. It falls under the SOLID acronym, which is a set of five principles aimed at making software designs more understandable, flexible, and maintainable.

DIP states that high-level modules should not depend on low-level modules. Both should depend on abstractions (e.g., interfaces). Further, abstractions should not depend on details. Details should depend on abstractions.

This design principle can improve the maintainability of a system in the following ways:

Decoupling of software modules: By having both high-level and low-level modules depend on the same abstraction, these modules become decoupled. Changes in one module won't affect the other directly. This makes maintenance easier since components can be modified separately.

Flexibility in component interchangeability: Given that it's the abstraction that glues modules together, different implementations of the abstraction can be plugged without changing the higher-level module. This allows for more flexibility in maintaining and expanding the system.

Enhanced testability: With abstractions between your components, you can provide test implementations or mocks for lower-level components to test higher-level ones in isolation. Therefore, making your system more maintainable with regard to testing.

Let's consider a simple example in the context of AWS Cloud Software Architecture. Suppose we have a higher-level module 'ReportGenerator', which depends on a lower-level module 'DataRetriever' to fetch data from an AWS RDS (Relational Database Service). If our system is designed without DIP, then any change in 'DataRetriever' or underlying RDS implementation would directly affect our 'ReportGenerator'.

However, if we design using DIP, we would create an interface 'IDataRetriever' and have both 'ReportGenerator' and 'DataRetriever' depend on this interface. 'DataRetriever' would implement this interface. As a result, even if we switch from AWS RDS to AWS DynamoDB (a NoSQL service), we can simply create 'DynamoDBDataRetriever' (a different implementation of 'IDataRetriever') without having to change 'ReportGenerator'. This is more maintainable as we didn't have to worry about changes rippling through the entire codebase.

To display this visually:

Without DIP:

```
ReportGenerator >-------> DataRetriever >-------> AWSService
```

With DIP:

```
ReportGenerator >-------> IDataRetriever
                               ^
                               |
                               |
                    DataRetriever >-------> AWSService
```

In conclusion, the Dependency Inversion Principle is crucial in promoting code maintainability in AWS Cloud Software Architecture by facilitating decoupling of components, enabling easier changes and fostering more effective testing.

How would you ensure that the Single Responsibility Principle is adhered to in a large project?

In software development, the Single Responsibility Principle (SRP) is part of the five SOLID principles that help in managing change, complexity, and interdependency in code. It states that a class should only have one reason to change, meaning that it should only have one job or responsibility.

Adhering to SRP in a large project is not a one-off exercise but a continuous one. It involves identifying potential design issues early and refactoring the code regularly as new features are added or existing features are changed.

Here some strategies to ensure that the SRP is adhered to in a large project:

1. **Break down large components into smaller ones:** In any large software project, it's possible to break down complex components into simpler, more manageable ones. Each sub-component can then be assigned to perform a single task. This not only ensures adherence to the single responsibility principle but also makes the software modules more readable, maintainable, and testable.

2. **Use code review practices:** Code review practices provide an additional layer of quality assurance above automated tests. A second pair of eyes on the code can help to ascertain whether a class or a function is doing more than it should be doing.

3. **Appropriately name classes and methods:** Properly naming classes and methods can give an indication of the responsibilities that class or method is taking on. If you can't easily represent the class or method behavior in its name, it might be a sign that it's doing too much.

4. **Write unit tests:** A class with single responsibility is typically easier to test, because you only need to cover one type of behavior. If you find that it's hard to write unit tests for a class, or that you need to mock a lot of dependencies, that's often an indication that a class is taking on too many responsibilities.

For example, let's consider designing an AWS cloud service architecture in which there is a class named 'EC2InstanceManager'. If this class is in charge of starting, stopping, monitoring, and also managing the security of instances, we are definitely violating the Single Responsibility Principle. Instead, it's better to split into several classes each with its own single responsibility - 'EC2InstanceStateManager' (for starting and stopping), 'EC2InstanceMonitor' (for monitoring), and 'EC2InstanceSecurityManager' (for managing security).

Note: Even though it's one of the essential principles of object-oriented design, the Single Responsibility Principle doesn't strictly apply only to classes or objects in a system. We can also apply it to software components, modules, subsystems, and services in an AWS cloud architecture - basically, anything that is a logical unit of code.

Can you give an example of a situation where it might be difficult to apply the Interface Segregation Principle?

The Interface Segregation Principle (ISP) is a part of SOLID principles which advocates for the segregation or the division of very large interfaces into smaller and more specific ones. This means that clients should not be forced to depend upon interfaces that they don' use.

Let's take an example to understand a scenario where implementing ISP might become complicated.

Think of a microservice architecture functioning in a cloud environment like AWS. You might create a centralized 'MicroserviceInterface' for other services to communicate with your microservice. This interface could have various methods related to numerous features such as:

'MicroserviceInterface':

```
interface MicroserviceInterface{
    method doTaskA();
    method doTaskB();
    method doTaskC();
    method doTaskD();
    ..
    ..
    method doTaskZ();
}
```

Other microservices are now forced to depend on the 'MicroserviceInterface' regardless of whether they need every feature or not.

A service 'ServiceOne' might only need the methods 'doTaskA', 'doTaskB', and 'doTaskC', while another service 'ServiceTwo' only uses 'doTaskY', 'doTaskZ'.

'ServiceOne' and 'ServiceTwo' are forced to have unnecessary dependencies because of the bulky 'MicroserviceInterface'.

ISP tells us to segregate this interface into smaller ones. But, when there are complex interdependencies between methods, implementing ISP could be challenging. A tough situation to apply ISP would be when a high degree of cohesion exists within the methods in the interface.

Let's say 'doTaskA', 'doTaskB', and 'doTaskC' in our 'MicroserviceInterface' are highly inter-dependent. They share common data, and perhaps, invocation of 'doTaskA' requires 'doTaskB' to have been invoked before.

If we segregate this into smaller interfaces as dictated by ISP, maintaining these dependencies could become hard. Data sharing might require extensive inter-service communication or place a heavy load on a service discovery network in a cloud environment like AWS.

This would be a situation where following Interface Segregation Principle might be complex, possibly leading to inefficient design as the interfaces are so inter-dependent.

In such cases, it might be better to stick with the monolithic interface and focus on other design principles. Or, re-evaluate the design of the interface and dependencies of the methods involved.

In essence, applying principles like SOLID should be driven by the context of the architecture, and the specific needs and constraints of the software being designed. It's important to remember that SOLID principles are guidelines rather than strict rules, and software architects possess the discretion to interpret and apply these principles as they see fit for their particular use case.

How do the SOLID principles aid in achieving a clean and scalable architecture?

The SOLID principles were established by Robert C. Martin, widely known as Uncle Bob, as a guideline for structuring an application in a maintainable and scalable way. The SOLID principles can contribute to producing clean architecture, especially in the context of cloud systems such as Amazon Web Services (AWS), by reducing dependencies, minimizing changes, and promoting extensibility among other benefits. Below, we'll delve into how each SOLID principle aids in creating efficient cloud systems.

1. **Single Responsibility Principle (SRP)**:

A class should have only one reason to change. This principle involves separating the concerns to narrow down the impact of future modifications. For instance, in AWS, Lambdas, which are essentially microservices, can be segregated on the basis of functionality like processing orders, inventory management, and user management. By doing this, changes to one microservice won't affect the others, enhancing the maintainability and reducing the risk of the system.

2. **Open/Closed Principle (OCP)**:

Software entities should be open for extension, but closed for modification. This principle advocates extending a system's behavior without altering its source code. For instance, adding a new AWS Lambda function instead of modifying an existing one. This principle reduces the risk introduced by changes and promotes the reusability of code.

3. **Liskov Substitution Principle (LSP)**:

Subtypes must be substitutable for their base types. In cloud systems, this could mean that, if an EC2 instance is slowing down due to high load, it can be replaced by another EC2 instance without any changes to the system.

4. **Interface Segregation Principle (ISP)**:

Clients should not be forced to depend on interfaces they do not use. For example, an AWS Lambda function that needs to write data to an S3 bucket shouldn't need to have permissions to access EC2 instances. By limiting unnecessary access, the system becomes more secure and less likely to have unexpected interactions.

5. **Dependency Inversion Principle (DIP)**:

Depend on abstractions, not on concrete classes. Instead of writing all code in a single monolithic application, using AWS Lambda, we can separate each function and develop individual Lambda functions. Each function will contain an interface and implementation part. The implementation part could change over time, but the interface remains the same. This way, high-level and low-level objects are not directly dependent on the concrete implementation refining the code reusability and adaptability.

In conclusion, adhering to SOLID principles can lead to a clean codebase (SRP, ISP), reduction in risk when making modifications (OCP), enhanced plug-and-play capacity (LSP), and less brittle and more stable code base with lower-level dependencies (DIP). This results in a more flexible, maintainable, understandable, and scalable AWS cloud architecture.

Can you describe a time when applying the SOLID principles significantly improved a project you were working on?

The SOLID principles (Single Responsibility, Open-Closed, Liskov Substitution, Interface Segregation, and Dependency Inversion) are design principles aimed at making software designs more understandable, easy to maintain and adaptable to change.

Consider a real-life example of a cloud-based eCommerce platform hosted on AWS. The initial design of the system didn't adhere to SOLID principles and was having performance and maintenance issues.

1. **Single Responsibility Principle (SRP)**: There was a monolithic service responsible for payments, inventory management, customer management, etc. This resulted in tightly coupled code. When a change was needed in one area, it often had implications elsewhere.

By applying the SRP, each service was made responsible for one thing only. For example, there was a separate service for payments, another for inventory management, etc. A change in one service was much less likely to affect others. It also helped with scalability, as services could be scaled independently based on demand.

2. **Open-Closed Principle (OCP)**: The system was not easy to extend. For instance, adding a new payment gateway required code changes and could potentially cause downtime.

After applying the OCP, services were made open for extension but closed for modification. Adding a new payment gateway became a case of implementing a new payment provider module, inserting this into the system, and seamlessly integrating with the payment service without modifying the existing codebase.

3. **Liskov Substitution Principle (LSP)**: There were issues related to extendibility. For example, each payment method should ideally be interchangeable without affecting the payment processing.

Adhering to the LSP, they created a base class with common payment method attributes and methods. Each specific payment method class then extended this base class, ensuring that any payment method could substitute any other without affecting behavior.

4. **Interface Segregation Principle (ISP)**: Clients were forced to depend on interfaces they didn't use, which can cause confusion and bloated classes.

By applying ISP, they redesigned interfaces to be client-specific. For example, the inventory service may interact with the payment service via a 'PaymentForInventory' interface that only includes methods relevant to inventory.

5. **Dependency Inversion Principle (DIP)**: Concretions were depended upon, making it hard to modify or test the code.

By applying the Dependency Inversion Principle, the high-level modules (like user interfaces or business logic) began depending on abstractions not on concretions. For instance, instead of the Order Management system interacting directly with the databases, it interacted with a Repository Interface (an abstraction). Using the DIP, it became easier to modify the code (just change the concrete classes) and also made unit testing easier as mock-ups could be used.

After applying the SOLID principles, the eCommerce platform became easier to maintain and extend, and could handle higher loads more reliably, leading to higher customer satisfaction and increased sales. The principles helped not only to resolve the existing issues but positioned the platform better for future improvements and adaptations.

How do the SOLID principles relate to other design principles like DRY (Don't Repeat Yourself) and YAGNI (You Ain't Gonna Need It)?

All SOLID, DRY, and YAGNI are design principles widely used in software development. While SOLID principles are primarily focused on making software design more understandable, flexible, and maintainable, DRY and YAGNI are general coding principles promoting better productivity and efficiency. Let us see how they relate with each other.

1. **SOLID and DRY:**

SOLID and DRY often go hand-in-hand as following one helps in adhering to the other.

Single Responsibility Principle (SRP): It states that a class should have one, and only one, reason to change. It directly aligns with DRY. By having each class do one thing, we are more likely to reuse it (keeping with DRY) without impacting other unrelated components.

Open/Closed Principle (OCP): It says classes should be open for extension but closed for modification. If a class has DRY code, it reduces the need to alter the class for new requirements because alterations will probably be incorporated in new derived classes, leading to the class remaining "Closed for modification".

Interface Segregation Principle (ISP): It involves splitting large interfaces into smaller and more specific ones, so clients will only have to know about the methods that are of interest to them. This, in turn, avoids duplication of code by implementing methods not needed by a class (DRY).

2. **SOLID and YAGNI:**

As for the YAGNI, there is a bit of perceived tension with SOLID, but they can coexist.

Liskov Substitution Principle (LSP): This principle can sometimes conflict with YAGNI because it encourages you to design your system in a future-proof way (consider all potential future subclasses), while YAGNI warns against over-engineering things we don't currently need. However, LSP makes the system more robust and prevents unexpected behaviors, which eventually reduces future changes.

Dependency Inversion Principle (DIP): This principle does not conflict with YAGNI directly. It is more about how we structure the code to make future changes more straightforward.

In summary, adhering to SOLID principles often naturally leads to DRY code, and while YAGNI might sometimes seem to conflict with SOLID, a carefully-balanced approach to both facilitates easy maintenance and future growth of the code.

Please note that these principles are guides for design and not absolute rules. Overly strict adherence to these principles can sometimes lead to unnecessary complexity or over-engineering. The understanding and balance of these principles tends to come with experience and knowledge of the problem domain.

Can you discuss some criticisms or limitations of the SOLID principles?

First, let's recall what SOLID stands for:

1. Single Responsibility Principle (SRP): A class should only handle a single functionality.

2. Open-Closed Principle (OCP): Software entities should be open for extension but closed for modification.

3. Liskov Substitution Principle (LSP): Objects in a program should be replaceable with instances of their subtypes without altering the correctness of that program.

4. Interface Segregation Principle (ISP): Clients should not be forced to depend on interfaces they do not use.

5. Dependency Inversion Principle (DIP): High-level modules should not depend on low-level modules. Both should depend on abstractions.

Now that we've reviewed the SOLID principles, let's discuss some of the criticisms and limitations.

1. **Over-engineering:** One of the common criticisms of SOLID is that it can lead to over-engineering in software design. For example, the SRP implies that each class should have only one functionality, which can lead to a proliferation of classes for what might be a rather simple piece of software.

2. **Procedural code:** SOLID principles are primarily related to

class-based or object-oriented programming, so it may not apply as much to other styles of coding like procedural or functional programming.

3. **Trade-off and Balance:** While SOLID principles are valuable in many cases, there are also situations where compromise or balance is required. For example, achieving ISP often requires violating SRP (i.e., if we segregate the interface well, it becomes necessary to include extra responsibilities in a single class).

4. **Learning curve:** The SOLID principles are quite abstract and can be difficult to comprehend for beginners.

5. **Principle Overlap:** There can be some overlaps between principles, especially between OCP and LSP. LSP can be achieved by applying OCP correctly. Similarly,DIP often needs to violate SRP to make a class depend on abstractions.

6. **Flexibility:** SOLID principles lessen the possibility of flexibility and surprise in the system. While these principles ensure code quality, they do so at the cost of discouraging unique solutions to certain problems.

7. **Time and Effort:** Applying SOLID principles is sometimes time-consuming because a perfectly SOLID system is time-consuming to build. It often requires a higher level of skill and dedication than creating a system that works but does not adhere to these principles.

Beyond these, it's worth remembering that these principles aren't laws. There can be occasions where it makes sense to ignore these principles for practical or pragmatic reasons. It's important to take them into context, consider what you're trying to achieve, and then decide if an exception is justified. It's always important not to be dogmatic about SOLID principles or any other rule in programming.

2.3 Creation of High-level Design Documents and Diagrams

What is the purpose of a high-level design document?

A high-level design document (HLLD), also known as a software architecture document or systems architecture document, serves as a high-level blueprint for how a software system or application will be structured and how it will function. It provides a visual overview of a system's architecture without diving into the minute implementation details.

The main purposes of a high-level design document include:

1. **System Overview**: It provides a holistic view of the software system, its main components and their interconnections.

2. **Communication**: It acts as a common language between various stakeholders (developers, project managers, customers, etc.) to ensure a shared understanding of the system.

3. **Guidance for Development Team**: It sets out the architectural vision for the development team and provides a guide for implementation.

4. **Facilitates Decision Making**: It aids in understanding the trade-offs of different design decisions and helps to justify them.

Specifically in the context of AWS Cloud, the high-level design document can include details about different AWS services to be used (like EC2, S3, Lambda, RDS, etc.), decision on multi-AZ or multi-region deployment strategies, choice of database and storage types, security considerations, monitoring solutions, to name a few.

Here is an example of a conceptual high-level design diagram:

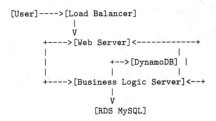

```
[User]---->[Load Balancer]
               |
               V
    +---->[Web Server]<------------+
    |                  |
    |            +-->[DynamoDB]  |
    |            |               |
    |    +---->[Business Logic Server]<--+
    |            |
    |            V
         [RDS MySQL]
```

It's critical to note that this is a simplified representation, the actual high-level design model would be far more complex, involving various AWS services interconnected in a specific manner based upon the use case and requirements.

What information should be included in a high-level design document?

A High-level Design (HLD) document gives a detailed conceptual understanding of the system. It gives an abstract view of the software architecture, components, modules, and their interactions. This information simplifies understanding the system functionality. Though the specific details may vary based on project requirements and the documenting style of the designing architect, an HLD generally includes the following details:

1. **Introduction and context:** This includes a brief overview of the project, the document's objective, scope, and stakeholders.

2. **System overview:** A brief description of the system which can include the problem statement, goal of the system, and high-level functionality.

3. **Architectural design:** This section presents the high-level architectural views of the system. This could include diagrams that map the system's main components, their relationships, and interactions. For example, you might include a graph such as:

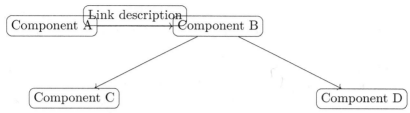

4. **System components:** This section contains detailed information about the primary software components. This part usually contains component diagrams or class diagrams.

5. **Database Design:** High-level design of the database schema, tables, relations, and an overview of how the data flows in the system.

6. **Interfaces and interactions:** This section should describe the system's interaction with other external systems. This could include descriptions of API calls and any dependencies expected from these external interfaces.

7. **Security:** Here you would outline any key security considerations or principles followed in the system design.

8. **Performance considerations:** This part identifies performance goals for the system and any high-level strategies for achieving them. This could include database indexing, caching strategy, etc.

9. **High-level risks:** Identifies potential risks or constraints that could impact the software's design or implementation.

An AWS high-level design would also include information about the key AWS services used in the design, and details about how they interact. Example services might include AWS Lambda for serverless computing, S3 for storage, and IAM for access management.

Remember, the purpose of the HLD is to present a broad perspective of the system architecture that serves as a blueprint for developing the system. It is not meant to describe implementation-level details, but rather provides the structure and the interrelationships upon which those details can be built.

How can UML (Unified Modeling Language) be used in creating design documents and diagrams?

Unified Modeling Language (UML) is a graphical notation that developers use for modeling software during the design phase of the software development life cycle. This graphical language can be utilized by software architects to create high-level design documents and diagrams that outline the structure, behavior, and more of a system.

The use of UML in the creation of high-level design documents pertains to the visual representation of the system's structure and behavior. It provides a way to describe the elements of a system, how they interact, and how they are organized, which is crucial for understanding complex systems.

Notable UML Diagrams used in high-level design include:

1. **Use Case Diagrams:** They represent the functionality of the system from an end-user's perspective. They depict the interaction between the system and external entities known as "actors". An actor represents a user or another system that will interact with the system under design.

2. **Class Diagrams:** They provide a static structure of the system, showcasing its classes, attributes, operations, and the relationships between the classes.

3. **Sequence Diagrams:** They emphasize the time ordering of messages which are sent and received between objects.

4. **Activity Diagrams:** They capture the dynamic behavior of the system. They express the workflow among the components of the system.

5. **Deployment Diagrams:** They describe the physical resources in a system, including nodes, components, and connections.

Example of a use case diagram:

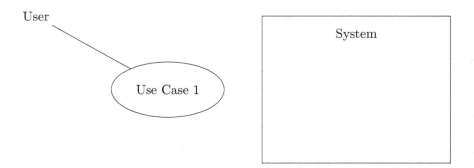

Example of a class diagram:

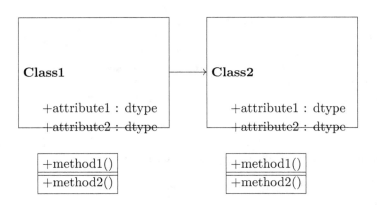

These diagrams can be used to create high-level design documents. The design documents can use the diagrams to show the logic flow between different components, the structure of the data, or the overall architecture of the system. With UML, system developers can understand the high-level design of the software, its components, their relationships, and their behavior more easily.

What is the difference between a sequence diagram and a class diagram?

In the context of Unified Modeling Language (UML), sequence diagrams and class diagrams are visualization tools that help in modeling, designing, and understanding the system better. Both diagrams serve different purposes and highlight different aspects of the system.

A sequence diagram is a type of interaction diagram that shows how objects interact in a specific order to realize a certain behavior of the system. It shows the flow of messages in the system and the life span of objects within use cases. Sequence diagrams are typically used to model the flow of logic within your system in response to external factors (like user actions).

A class diagram, on the other hand, is a type of structure diagram that describes the static structure of a system by showing the system's classes, their attributes and methods, and the relationships between the classes. Class diagrams are used to model the basic structure and the static semantics of an object-oriented system. They don't show the temporal sequence of interactions (which is what sequence diagrams do).

So in essence, class diagrams depict the static elements of the system while sequence diagrams expose the dynamic logic of the system.

Here's a simple comparison in the terms of math notations:

- A class diagram might be represented symbolically as a set of entities 'E = e_1, e_2, ..., e_n' and the relationships between them 'R = r_1, r_2, ..., r_n', with each 'r' indicating some form of relationship, such as inheritance, association, or dependency, among the entities 'e'.

- A sequence diagram might be represented as a sequence or an ordered set where the order matters 'S = s_1, s_2, ..., s_n', where each 's' is an interaction between or among entities. They represent an exchange of control and information.

How do you ensure that design documents are kept up-to-date as a project evolves?

Ensuring the accuracy and currency of high-level design documents and diagrams as a project evolves can be a challenging aspect of software architecture, especially in an AWS Cloud context. Here are several strategies that can be employed:

1. **Version Control System**: A Version Control System (VCS), such as Git, can be beneficial for maintaining design documents up-to-date. It allows tracking changes in the project and can be used to manage versions of design documents and diagrams. AWS provides CodeCommit, a fully-managed source control service that hosts secure Git-based repositories.

2. **Continuous Documentation**: Continual documentation is as important as continuous integration. This practice involves frequently updating documentation as the system is designed, developed, and evolved. AWS Quicksight can be used as a tool to keep diagrams and other visual representations updated. Changes in services can be updated in real time, giving you a current depiction of your architecture.

3. **Using Automated Tools**: Automated documentation tools can be very useful for reflecting the changes in the system quickly in the design documents as well. Tools such as AWS CloudFormation Designer and AWS CDK (Cloud Development Kit) can be utilised for the purpose.

4. **Scheduled Reviews And Updates**: Regular schedules for reviewing the design documents can be set up. During these sessions, the team can check if the documents still match the current state of the system and then update them if necessary.

5. **Assigning Responsibility**: Assign a specific person or team with the responsibility to ensure consistency between the project and its documentation. Having a dedicated AWS team to ensure this can help in a big way.

6. **Collaboration and Communication**: It is also important to foster a collaborative culture where teams are communicating and collaborating effectively to ensure a single source of truth.

Given the potential complexities of software architecture diagrams, the right strategies and tools are crucial for maintaining up-to-date, accurate, and useful design documentation.

How can design documents and diagrams facilitate communication within a development team?

High-level design documents and diagrams play a crucial role in software development projects, particularly in facilitating communication within a development team. They serve as a tangible representation of systems and interconnections that can be very complex when only described verbally or textually. Here are several ways these tools can aid communication:

1. Provides a common understanding: The initial stage of any project involves a lot of brainstorming and discussion about the proposed system or application. High-level design documents and diagrams turn these abstract ideas into concrete models which every team member can understand. They provide a clear visualisation of the software architecture, components, and the flow of data, which helps prevent miscommunication and confusion later in the project.

2. Acts as a reference resource: They serve as a baseline or reference for the developers during the coding stage. The team members can refer back to these documents to recall how a particular module was supposed to function or to solve disagreements about the design.

3. Helps in updating and maintaining the system: These documents provide deep insight into past design decisions and system operations, making them invaluable for future maintenance and modifications. For example, if a bug surfaces after the software has been deployed, engineers can consult the documents to identify the problem and understand its root cause.

4. Streamlines the onboarding process: For new team members or external stakeholders, these diagrams can provide a quick and comprehensive overview of the system's structure and functionality. Instead of going through extensive documentation, new additions to the team can get up to speed more quickly.

In terms of AWS Cloud Software Architecture, high-level design documents can include diagrams such as System Context diagrams to identify external entities that interact with the system, Container diagrams to illustrate the high-level technology choices, Component diagrams to detail the division of software or services, and AWS Architecture diagrams to show the configuration of AWS services.

The lack of these architectural diagrams within a team could lead to misunderstandings about the system's design or operation leading to inefficiencies, and potential errors in the final product.

Can you describe a situation where a high-level design document significantly impacted the outcome of a project?

A High-Level Design Document (HLDD) describes the system's architecture in a broad perspective. It focuses on the structure and interaction between software components but not the inner details of components. In AWS Cloud Software Architecture, HLDD is critical in design and implementation.

Here is an example of a previous project where high-level design documents significantly affected the outcome:

The project was about designing a Multi-Tenant Cloud-Based Software as a Service (SaaS) Application on AWS. Since there are multiple tenants, each with different operational and data isolation requirements, the project's complexity was high. Given the intricacy of the task, it was crucial to document the high-level design to make sure all stakeholders (like developers, project managers, and other architects) have a common understanding of the architecture's overall view.

The high-level design document comprised the following AWS components:

- Amazon EC2 (virtual servers in the cloud)
- AWS RDS (Relational Database Service for database management)
- Amazon DynamoDB (for NoSQL database services)
- AWS S3 (Scalable storage in the cloud)
- Amazon SNS (Simple Notification Service for sending notifications)
- AWS IAM (Identity and Access Management for secure access)

Without the use of high-level design document, it would have been challenging for every stakeholder to understand how these components would interact in a scalable, secure and performant way.

Here is a high-level design diagram:

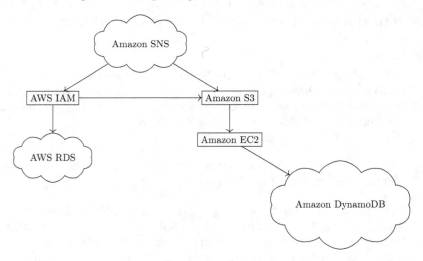

In the above diagram, direct interactions between the components are denoted by bidirectional arrows while indirect interactions are shown by unidirectional arrows.

The creation of high-level design documents was a significant part of this project. This not only refined the architectural vision for the project but also streamlined the entire implementation process. The team could evaluate each design decision based on the shared understanding of systems, which resulted in improved design quality and reduced time to troubleshoot. In this way, the high-level design document significantly impacted the project's success.

What is a component diagram and what information does it convey?

A component diagram, in the context of AWS Cloud Software Architecture, is a type of structural diagram that showcases the software components present within a system along with their interrelationships. In this context, a "component" usually refers to a major subsystem or module within a software system.

The key information conveyed by a component diagram includes:

1. **Components**: These are the main functional units of a system. They are depicted as rectangles within the diagram. Components could represent software modules, classes, objects, etc.

2. **Interfaces**: Interfaces describe the "contracts" between different components. They can encompass announced services, expected services, and so on. They are represented with circles or semi-circles.

3. **Relationships**: These represent connections between different components. They could represent dependencies, communications, or invoking relationships.

4. **Ports**: Ports are used to encapsulate the components and decouple them from their environment. They help establish a barrier that protects the inner implementation of a component from being affected by environmental changes.

In AWS terms, a component like an EC2 instance could represent a component that communicates with others like S3, DynamoDB, or an internal microservice via a load balancer (interface).

Here's an example of how a component diagram might look like:

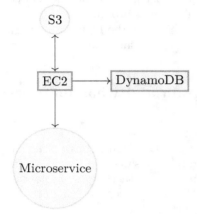

In this diagram, EC2 instance (main component) interacts with S3 (using an outbound interface), DynamoDB (inbound interface), and a microservice (bi-directional interface).

Overall, a component diagram in AWS Cloud Software Architecture serves the purpose of visualizing the structural organization of the system components and their interactions. It also aids in understanding data flow, dependencies, and various interfaces.

How do you approach the task of creating a design document for a large and complex system?

Creating a design document for large and complex systems requires a methodical approach. Amazon Web Services (AWS), suggesting a well-architected framework provides a great toolset for software architects to design robust, secure, efficient, and cost-effective systems.

Here are the major steps involved in creating a design document:

1. **Understanding Requirements and Constraints**: It's critical to gather and analyze the business and technical requirements, the budget constraints, the target users, and the performance expectations. AWS provides services like AWS Cost Explorer and AWS TCO Calculator to assist in understanding costs. AWS service quotas can be used to understand the limitations of each AWS service to ensure they align with your application needs.

2. **Defining System's Functional Components** It's equally crucial to articulate all the different components of the system and describe their functionality. AWS allows you to categorize your system into several categories such as compute (e.g. EC2, Lambda), storage (e.g. S3, EBS), databases (e.g. RDS, DynamoDB), networking & content delivery (VPC, Route 53, CloudFront), Developer tools(AWS CodeStar, AWS Cloud9), Management & governance (CloudWatch, Systems Manager), etc.

3. **Mapping Functional Components to AWS Services** Once you have outlined your functional components, map them to the relevant AWS services. For example, if your system's functional requirement is to process data in real time, you can use services such as Kinesis Data Streams.

4. **Identifying Data Flow** Describing how data flows between different components of the system is of the utmost importance. AWS has tools likeAWS Step Functions that assist in visualizing the components and data flow of your system.

5. **Identify Security Requirements** You should design your architecture keeping security in mind. For example, you could use AWS Identity and Access Management (IAM) to control the access to AWS services and resources. AWS Key Management Service (KMS) can be used to create and manage cryptographic keys and control their use across a wide range of AWS services and in your applications.

6. **High-Level Architecture Diagram** Creating a high-level architecture diagram is a visual way of representing your system. The

AWS Architecture Center provides reference architecture diagrams, vetted architecture solutions, AWS Well-Architected best practices, patterns, and icons, that can be used to create these diagrams.

Designing a large complex system would require breaking down the system components into the smallest possible units (microservices) and designing for each of those. In microservices architecture, a complex application is broken down into smaller, independent applications. These services run in their own processes and communicate with each other using APIs.

Let's consider an example of an e-commerce application that includes user management, inventory management, payment processing, and shipping services. The high-level design might look something like this:

User Management	Inventory Management	Payment Processing	Shipping Service
↓	↓	↓	↓
Lambda	DynamoDB	API Gateway	S3

Arrows indicate the direction of data flow and the AWS services that correspond to the system's functional components. Use of other AWS services like Amazon CloudFront (for content delivery), AWS Systems Manager (for automation), AWS IAM (for access control), Amazon CloudWatch (for logging and monitoring), etc., would also be captured in the detailed version of the design document.

The design document should be comprehensive enough to provide adequate details to all stakeholders, which includes not just the development team but also managers, clients, and any third-party reviewers.

Can you discuss some strategies for making design documents clear and understandable to all stakeholders?

When creating high-level design documents and diagrams, the primary goal is to convey the system's architecture in a digestible manner to all stakeholders involved, including both technical and non-technical members.

1. **Simplicity and clarity**: High-level design documents should be free from any technical jargon that only team members can understand. Use laymen's terms whenever needed and appropriate. The use of clear language is paramount in communication.

2. **Object-Oriented Analysis (OOA)**: Leverage this strategy for a visual representation that all team members can understand. Using the Unified Modeling Language (UML), your team can create these high-level diagrams. Here is an example of a simple UML class diagram:

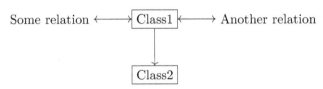

3. **Use of Architectural Patterns**: Reusable solutions to commonly occurring problems in software architecture (like microservices or layered architecture) can be helpful. You can mention these patterns to quickly describe the system's high-level design.

4. **Show relationships**: Diagrams should convey, at a glance, how various systems or software components interact. You might use arrows, flowcharts, and other elements to signal these relationships.

5. **Modularity**: Break down your design into multiple modules, subsystems, or components. This way, stakeholders can conceptualize each piece in isolation and in relation to the whole.

6. **Annotations and Documentation**: Always annotate your diagrams, providing descriptions of components, database entities, or business processes. Also, include a guide or key explaining your symbols, colors, or arrows.

7. **Feedback and Iteration**: Gather feedback from stakeholders and revise the document accordingly. An unclear document could lead to misunderstandings, incorrect assumptions, and eventual project failure.

8. **Tool Selection**: Use suitable tools for creating these diagrams (like AWS Architecture Diagrams, Lucidchart, draw.io, or Microsoft Visio). Easy-to-use tools improve the process of creating, modifying, and sharing your design documents.

Remember, the role of these design documents and diagrams is to foster a shared understanding among all stakeholders involved in the project.

2.4   Making Technology Stack Decisions

What factors do you consider when choosing a technology stack for a new project?

Choosing a technology stack for a new project is based on various factors. Three key considerations are: the project requirements, the team's proficiency with the technology, and the quality of support and ecosystem for the chosen technology. But, these are not limited. There are several other factors including project scale, cost, time to market, future expansion and maintainability. So let's dive down into these factors:

1. **Project Requirements:** The nature of your project has a high impact on the technology choice you make. For instance, if you're building a simple web app, a full-fledged monolithic framework like

Django or Rails might be overkill. A lighter framework like Flask or Express could suffice. However, if you're building a large-scale enterprise application, you'd need a robust framework and supporting services which can handle complex scenarios and heavy loads. This might necessitate a service oriented or microservice architecture, which AWS Beanstalk or AWS Fargate can provide.

2. **Team's Proficiency:** It's vital to choose a technology stack that your development team is familiar with. For instance, if your team has experience with Python, a stack with Django or Flask would be easier to work with. If they are skilled with Java, a stack with SpringBootApplication could be more appropriate.

3. **Quality of Support and Ecosystem:** The productivity of your team and the sustainability of your application depends on the developer community, ecosystem, and official support for your technology choice. It is generally advisable to go with technologies that have a strong community, mature ecosystem, and active development. For instance, AWS has a very wide community, and provides robust support for developers and users.

4. **Scalability:** Depending on the expected load on your application, you'd want to consider whether the technology stack can handle scaling. Both vertical scaling (increasing server size) and horizontal scaling (increasing server count) should be possible. Solutions like AWS Elastic Beanstalk or AWS EC2 with load balancing provide easy scalability.

5. **Cost:** The cost of technology is also a factor. You should consider both the direct costs (such as licensing costs, if any) and the indirect costs (like the development and maintenance costs).

6. **Time to Market:** Some stacks allow rapid development, which could be vital if you want to launch quickly. For instance, Ruby on Rails is known for its principle of Convention Over Configuration, which facilitates rapid development.

7. **Future Expansion and Maintenance:** You also need to consider the ease of maintenance and future expansion possibilities of

the technology.

Here's a flowchart representation of some of these decisions:

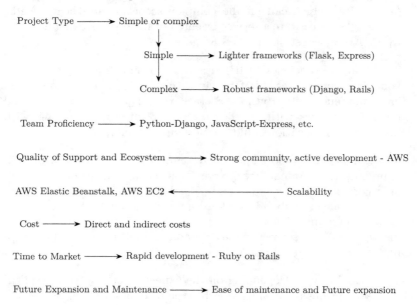

Remember, the objective is to define a technology stack that suits your particular project, and there's no one-size-fits-all solution. Deciding on your tech stack is a critical decision that will influence your project's workflow and overall success. At the same time, being flexible and open to change is essential, given the rapidly evolving technology landscape.

How would you decide between using a relational database and a NoSQL database for a particular application?

The decision to use a relational database (RDBMS) or a NoSQL database typically depends on the specific use-case of the application

CHAPTER 2. SOFTWARE ARCHITECTURE PRINCIPLES

you're developing, the data model you're working with, the scalability requirements, and the nature of operations the database needs to perform. Understanding the trade-offs of both database formats can help you make an informed decision.

1. **Data Model**: A relational database is best used when there are complex relationships between entities and the data's structure is fairly consistent and clear. It models data as tables, and leverages SQL for interacting with data. RDBMS systems like MySQL, PostgreSQL, Oracle, and the AWS offering, Amazon RDS, are industrial-grade databases suitable for enterprise software.

Conversely, NoSQL databases are designed to handle unstructured data and are easily scalable. They handle four major types of data models: key-value, document, column-oriented, and graph. AWS DynamoDB (key-value and document) and AWS Neptune (graph) are examples of NoSQL databases.

2. **Scalability**: If your application requires horizontal scalability or will deal with large volumes of data, a NoSQL database might provide more flexibility. NoSQL databases are designed to be distributed across multiple machines, making it easier to grow by adding more machines to the network. Examples of highly scalable NoSQL databases include MongoDB and Cassandra.

3. **Transactions**: If your application requires complex transactions with multiple operations, particularly where ACID (Atomicity, Consistency, Isolation, Durability) properties are necessary, RDBMS would be the right choice. Most NoSQL solutions do not fully support ACID properties and instead focus on eventual consistency.

4. **Speed**: If fast reads and writes are important (without requiring complex joins or multi-row transactions), NoSQL databases offer faster operations. For instance, AWS DynamoDB is designed to handle high velocity reads and writes.

Therefore, the decision boils down to analyzing the application's data characteristics and requirements in terms of structure, scalability, consistency, and speed. More complex requirements may even war-

	RDBMS	NoSQL
Data Model	Structured, tables	Unstructured, flexible
Scalability	Vertical scaling by adding more power (CPU, RAM)	Horizontal scaling by adding more machines
Transactions	Supports ACID properties	More focused on CAP theorem, eventual consistency
Speed	Optimized for complex queries with joins	Optimized for single row operations, fast reads/writes

rant a hybrid approach using both types of databases.

Here's a tabular comparison for easy reference:

However, it should be kept in mind that these are general guidelines and the right decision heavily depends on the specific use cases. The line between NoSQL and RDBMS is also increasingly blurred as more features are added to both types of systems. For example, NoSQL solutions have begun to support more complex querying and transactions, while RDBMS solutions have increased their capabilities around replication, partitioning, and scalability.

Can you discuss some pros and cons of different backend programming languages (e.g., Java, Python, Node.js)?

Each backend programming language has distinct advantages and disadvantages depending on the use case, scalability needs, and complexity of the project. Below, are the high-level pros and cons of Java, Python, and Node.js:

Java:

Java, an object-oriented programming language, offers platform independence because of its "Write once, Run anywhere" paradigm. Java is used heavily in enterprise-scale applications, JVM offers a robust ecosystem and Java offers built-in support for multithreading.

Pros:

- *Robustness*: Java is strongly typed and has automatic garbage collection, allowing management of memory allocation.

- *Platform independent:* Java is designed to run on any platform with the JVM (Java Virtual Machine), without recompilation.

- *Scalability:* Java can manage heavy traffic and large-scale projects.

Cons:

- *Verbose and complex syntax:* Java could be overwhelming for new programmers because it requires writing a lot of code even for simple tasks.

- *Performance:* While Java is a powerful language, it's slower compared to languages like C++.

Python:

Python is renowned for its simplicity and readability. It is widely used in scientific computing, data mining, machine learning, and AI projects.

Pros:

- *Easy Syntax:* Python's emphasis on code readability, simplicity, and clear syntax makes it a great language for beginners.

- *Strong for Machine Learning and Data Science:* Python has a large selection of libraries like NumPy, Pandas, and others.

- *Rapid Prototyping:* Python allows for quick solution implementation compared to other languages, which makes it suitable for startups and prototype development.

Cons:

- *Speed Limitations:* Python is slower compared to languages like Java or C++.

- *Not Native to Mobile Environment:* Python is often not the go-to language for mobile app development.

Node.js:

Node.js isn't a language, but a runtime that allows Javascript to run on the server side. It's built on Chrome's V8 JavaScript engine.

Pros:

- *High Performance:* Node.js has an event-driven architecture and asynchronous I/O, these design choices optimize throughput and scalability in web applications that have many I/O operations.

- *Shared Language:* On both client-side and server-side, Javascript can be used, enhancing efficiency.

- *Large Ecosystem:* NPM (Node Package Manager) is the world's largest software registry that has numerous handy tools available and ready to use.

Cons:

- *Callback Hell:* Asynchronous programming leads to complex, nested callbacks, leading to unmanageable code, although this can be mitigated with Promises and async/await.

- *Not Suitable for CPU-intensive tasks:* Node.js is not suitable for heavy computational tasks that can block incoming requests, leading to substantial slowdowns.

Therefore, when choosing a backend language, you must consider the project requirements. If it's a large, enterprise-scale application, Java may be preferred. For AI-related, data analysis or rapid prototyping, Python may be a better choice. If the project is I/O heavy and would benefit from non-blocking requests and sharing code between server and client, then Node.js might be advantageous.

How does the choice of technology stack impact the scalability and maintainability of a system?

The choice of a technology stack can significantly impact the scalability and maintainability of a system. Each technology stack comes with its own set of benefits and trade-offs that can influence a system's ability to scale and be maintained over time.

Scalability is the ability of a system to handle increased workload without compromising performance. When choosing a technology stack, factors such as support for horizontal and vertical scaling, distributed architecture, and concurrent processing capability can influence the scalability of the system.

For instance, using a microservices-based architecture such as AWS Lambda would provide higher scalability compared to a monolithic architecture, as services can be scaled independently depending on the workload. In contrast, if you are using a relational database like MySQL, it might be more challenging to scale because it doesn't support horizontal scaling (adding more nodes to the system) as seamlessly as NoSQL databases like DynamoDB do.

The ability to use auto-scaling features provided by cloud platforms like AWS also depends on the technology stack. For example, Java applications can use AWS's EC2 Auto Scaling and Elastic Beanstalk, while applications that use serverless technologies can use AWS Lambda's Provisioned Concurrency or AWS's Fargate in the case of containerized applications.

Maintainability refers to the ease with which a software system can be understood, repaired, or enhanced. It's affected by factors such as the complexity of the technology, the quality of documentation, availability of skills in the market, the strength of community support, the maturity of the technology, etc.

Let's take Python as an example language that is widely recognized for its readability, simplicity, and extensive libraries and frameworks, which contribute to high maintainability. On the other hand, a language like C++ may offer powerful features, but it can be more complex and harder to maintain.

Each technology in the stack should follow the principles of "Separation of Concerns," meaning that each part of the stack should deal with a specific task. Mixing layers or using technologies that are not well-suited for a task makes the system more complex and harder to maintain.

There's no one-size-fits-all answer to this question; the right technology stack heavily depends on the specific project requirements, existing team knowledge, and other factors.

However, here's a format to consider when comparing different stacks:

Technology Stack	Scalability	Maintainability
Stack 1	High/Low/Medium	High/Low/Medium
Stack 2	High/Low/Medium	High/Low/Medium
Stack 3	High/Low/Medium	High/Low/Medium

Remember to adapt the actual evaluation to the needs and constraints of each project.

How do you keep up-to-date with new technologies and evaluate whether they're worth adopting?

Keeping up-to-date with new technologies, especially in a field as dynamic and fast-paced as cloud computing, can be challenging. However, as an AWS Cloud Software Architect, it's important to consistently explore new technologies, standards, and tools to drive continuous innovation, improvement, and efficiency within your organization. Here are few ways that you can keep up-to-date:

1. **Participate in Professional Communities and Networks:** On-

line forums, social media groups, and in-person meetups allow you to collaborate and learn from other professionals in your field. For example, the AWS Developer Community is a vibrant platform where you can interact with other AWS users and experts.

2. **Attend Tech Conferences and Webinars:** These events can provide deep insights into emerging trends, technologies, best practices, and case studies. AWS re:Invent, AWS Summit, and many other tech conferences are great places to gain knowledge and interact with peers.

3. **Training and Certifications:** AWS Training and Certification builds your competence, confidence, and credibility through practical cloud skills that help you innovate and build your future.

4. **Follow Blogs, Podcasts, and Newsletters:** Many tech companies and experts share their insights, experiences, and expertise through these channels.

5. **Vendor Documentation and Resources:** AWS, for instance, often publishes whitepapers, guides, and case studies which can help you stay updated with their newest offerings.

When it comes to evaluating whether a new technology is worth adopting, some key questions to consider might include:

- Will it provide significant benefits compared to our current solution (e.g., in terms of scalability, performance, reliability, security)?

- How well does it integrate with our existing technology stack?

- What is the learning curve associated with it and do we have the necessary skills and resources to handle it?

- What is the total cost of ownership?

Consider using a decision matrix, or a similar decision-making tool, to help evaluate different options against various criteria. Here's an example of a simple decision matrix:

	Criteria 1	Criteria 2	Criteria 3
Technology A	4	5	2
Technology B	2	3	4
Technology C	5	1	3

Each cell in the matrix represents a score (from 1 to 5) indicating how well each technology meets each criterion. Note that a more thorough assessment might involve assigning different weights to different criteria based on their relative importance within your specific context.

You should also consider conducting a proof of concept or pilot project to gain hands-on experience with the technology and more accurately assess its potential value and fit.

Remember, just because a technology is new does not necessarily mean it is better or it is suited to your business needs. Having a methodical approach to evaluating new technologies will help mitigate the risk of adoption while ensuring that you continue to innovate and improve your technology stack.

Can you discuss a time when the choice of technology stack significantly affected a project you were working on?

An organization decided to move its physical infrastructure to the AWS Cloud. The technology stack that needed to be built comprised many services like Amazon S3, EC2, Lambda, RDS, DynamoDB, and IAM, along with other AWS services. The team had initially decided on using EC2-based compute architecture.

However, after initial development, they found that managing the EC2 instances was complex and time-consuming because they needed to update, patch, monitor, and handle scalability. Additionally, the cost of running servers full time was proving to be expensive, even though they were not utilized to their maximum capacity.

This situation needed re-evaluation, and considering serverless compute architecture was beneficial. Serverless architecture using AWS Lambda could potentially resolve these issues, as developers wouldn't have to manage servers, and they would pay only for the compute time they consume.

After switching to AWS Lambda, the developers found it more effective, efficient, and cost-effective. An implication also was that developers could work more on the product's core features rather than managing servers.

This example demonstrates that the choice of the appropriate technology stack is crucial because it directly affects project development, ongoing management, cost, and overall project success. The selection of the right AWS services as part of the technology stack should be made based on specific use case requirements, the skills of the team, cost constraints, and long-term scalability and maintainability.

How do you assess the learning curve of a new technology for the development team?

Assessing the learning curve of a new technology for a development team involves evaluating several parameters. These parameters could include the team's existing skillset, the complexity of the technology, the availability of learning resources, and the adaptability of the team.

1. **Team's Existing Skillset**: A team that's experienced in similar technology or the underlying principles will have a less steep learning curve compared to one that's new to the domain. For instance, if your team has a good grasp of Python and you are considering a tool that uses Python scripts, the learning curve would be less steep compared to starting with a completely new programming language.

2. **Complexity of the Technology**: The complexity of the technology itself is a big factor. Technologies that are intuitive, well-

architected, and follow established design principles will be easier to learn compared to ones that are convoluted or poorly designed.

3. **Availability of Learning Resources**: Technologies that have well-documented learning resources, such as online tutorials, developer communities, Q&A forums, are easier to pick up. The presence of a strong and supportive community can significantly flatten the learning curve.

4. **Adaptability of the Team**: Some teams are simply more adaptable to new technologies due to the culture, mindset, or experience of the team members. A team that embraces a learning culture may find it easier to grasp a new technology.

Keep in mind the technology stack decision-making is not only about the learning curve but also about trade-offs in performance, functionality, scalability, and cost. Even if a technology has a steep learning curve, it might be worth it if it provides significant advantages in these other areas.

What is the role of legacy systems in deciding a technology stack?

The technology stack of a project or an organization often refers to the combination of software tools, programming languages, and technologies that are used in the development and deployment of websites, apps, and other digital products. When referring to legacy systems, we mean the existing or older technology, software systems, and processes that a business still uses, despite them being eclipsed by newer, often superior, technologies.

Legacy systems occupy a significant role in deciding a technology stack for several reasons:

1. **Interoperability**: New technology must often coexist, integrate and synchronize with the existing legacy systems to ensure seamless operations. This capability can rule out certain technologies that lack

interoperability with the existing legacy systems.

2. **Migration Cost**: The decision to adopt new technologies is sometimes made difficult by the cost (money, time, human resources) involved in migrating from a legacy system to a new system. This cost can be in terms of employing new staff, training existing staff, downtime during migration, potential loss of data, etc. This cost must be factored into the decision to adopt a new stack.

3. **Productivity**: Sometimes, the benefit of maintaining a team's productivity by keeping to familiar (legacy) systems offsets the benefits of a new technology stack. Organizational knowledge about a particular technology can be a valuable asset that is disrupted when a new stack is adopted.

4. **Security**: Newer systems, while offering potential benefits in terms of performance, may not have been tested extensively in the field and may present unforeseen vulnerabilities. Existing legacy systems may be well understood in terms of their security profile and are considered a safer bet.

5. **Technical Debt**: The legacy system may carry associated technical debt that needs to be addressed in adopting the new technology stack. Choices might be limited to technologies that allow this debt to be paid off.

6. **Strategic Impact**: The legacy system could have strategic impacts including supplier agreements, long-term customer contracts, and regulatory obligations. These factors could limit the options for changing the technology stack.

In the end, the decision to adopt a new technology stack must factor in the impact on, and fit with, existing legacy systems. The systems' interoperability, performance, scalability, and maintainability with the legacy system are critical factors for consideration.

Can you discuss some trade-offs in choosing a monolithic architecture vs. a microservices architecture?

Both monolithic and microservices architectures have benefits, drawbacks, and contexts where they excel. The decision on which to adopt will depend on your team's capabilities, your project requirements, and your tolerance for complexity.

Monolithic Architecture

A monolith is a software application whose components are interconnected and interdependent, as opposed to a microservices design where individual components are separated and communicate via APIs.

Pros:

1. **Simplicity**: Monolithic applications are easier to develop, test, and debug because everything is in a single codebase. They also normally have fewer cross-cutting concerns, such as authorization and rate limiting.

2. **Consistency**: They may be easier to manage because they are a single system. Development and operations teams do not have to worry about managing and coordinating multiple services.

3. **Performance**: There are no service boundaries, so accessing different functionalities in the system can be faster because local function calls are typically faster than inter-process communication (IPC).

Cons:

1. **Scalability**: Monolithic applications can become complex and difficult to manage, as functionalities are added. Scaling becomes more challenging because you can't just scale the parts of the system that are under heavy load.

2. **Technology Stack Flexibility**: Monoliths are typically built

using a single technology stack, which can limit the ability to use the right tool for the job.

3. **Dependability**: If a part of the system fails, the entire system is impacted.

Microservices Architecture

Microservices architecture involves developing an application as a suite of small services, each running in its own process and communicating with lightweight mechanisms, often an HTTP resource API. These services are built around business capabilities and independently deployable by fully automated deployment machinery.

Pros:

1. **Scalability**: Each microservice can be scaled independently to meet demand for that service. This enables cost-effective utilization of resources.

2. **Flexibility and Agility**: Microservices can be written using different technology stacks, can be managed by different teams, and can be updated independently of each other.

3. **Reliability**: Since each service is isolated and independent, failure in one does not directly impact others.

Cons:

1. **Complexity**: Microservices introduce complexity in terms of service orchestration, inter-service communication, data consistency, and operational overhead.

2. **Performance**: Service boundaries typically introduce latency due to the need for serialization, network congestion, etc.

3. **Data Integrity**: Maintaining data consistency across services can be a major challenge.

4. **Operational Overhead**: Each service has its runtime, which

consumes resources. There may also be an increased burden on operations and infrastructure teams to manage multiple services.

Undeniably, there isn't one right answer when choosing between monolithic and microservices architectures. The decision should not purely be based on trends or big-name adoptions but on your individual project needs, team skills, and long-term plans. The best approach might be to start with a monolithic structure for simplicity, and as your application grows more complex, begin breaking it down into microservices where it makes sense to do so.

Please note that there's a concept known as the "Monolithic First" coined by Martin Fowler, which suggests that microservice architecture should be the last resort and one should start development with a monolithic architecture, only considering microservices when they face problems associated with the monolithic architecture. However, it is not universally accepted and should be evaluated on a case-by-case basis.

How would you decide between different cloud service providers (e.g., AWS, Google Cloud, Azure) for a particular project?

When deciding between different cloud service providers such as AWS, Google Cloud, and Azure for a particular project, there are several factors that one should consider.

1. **Type of Service Offerings**: Different service providers have different service offerings. Some have strengths in certain areas compared to others. For example, AWS offers the largest variety of services, followed by Azure and Google Cloud. AWS has strengths in areas such as databases, containers, machine learning, among others. Google Cloud has strengths in areas such as AI and machine learning and provides a robust big data platform. Azure, on the other hand, tightly integrates with other Microsoft products and is often preferred for organizations relying heavily on Microsoft for other IT needs.

2. **Cost**: The cost is another factor to consider. These providers offer different pricing models depending on the services. AWS, for example, offers pay-as-you-go, save when you reserve, and pay less by using more models. Azure provides pay-as-you-go and short-term commitments with the option of reserved instances for long-term. Google Cloud uses a similar model with the additional benefit of automatic discounted prices for long-term usage.

3. **Performance**: Another key area of focus is the performance or speed that the cloud service providers offer. For instance, Google Cloud has an edge when it comes to network speed as it leverages Google's global fiber network. However, for compute capabilities, it can be subjective and often dependent on the specific use-case or location.

4. **Security**: All these services provide robust security mechanisms. However, the level of control and features differ based on the cloud provider. AWS, for example, provides a wide range of mechanisms to enhance security.

5. **Integration**: The ability to integrate with existing systems is another factor. For example, if the project largely uses Microsoft products, Azure could be a preferred choice due to the ease of integration.

6. **Scalability**: Cloud service providers also differ in scalability. In this regard, AWS offers more scalability options followed by Azure and Google Cloud.

7. **Response Development Cycle**: Google Cloud and Azure provide faster development cycles allowing faster product completion.

8. **Server Locations**: Depending on the need for latency, data sovereignty, and other factors, the number, and spread of data centers globally can also be a determining factor.

A detailed analysis with a weighting matrix, rating, and comparing several factors between providers can help in making the decision.

For example:

```
| Factors         | AWS  | Google Cloud | Azure  |
|-----------------|------|--------------|--------|
| Services        | 5    | 3            |4       |
| Cost            | 4    | 5            | 3      |
| Performance     | 4    | 5            | 4      |
| Security        | 5    | 4            | 5      |
| Integration     | 5    | 4            | 5      |
| Scalability     | 5    | 4            | 4      |
| Dev Cycle       | 3    | 5            | 5      |
| Server Location | 5    | 4            | 5      |
```

Based on the ratings and the importance assigned to each factor, a decision can be made. The business requirements and priorities will ultimately dictate which cloud service provider will be the best fit for a particular project.

It's also worth noting that multicloud strategies are becoming increasingly popular, where companies do not exclusively align with a single cloud provider but take advantages of the strengths of each.

Therefore, the decision to choose the right cloud provider is both a technical and a business decision that must be taken with due diligence.

2.5   Ensuring System Scalability, Reliability, Security, and Maintainability

What strategies can be used to ensure system scalability?

System scalability refers to a system's capacity to handle increased workload by continually improving performance as resources (like CPU, memory, and storage) are added. Ensuring system scalability in AWS cloud architecture can be achieved by implementing several strategies, including:

1. **Elasticity and Auto-scaling**: This strategy involves automatically scaling resource capacity up or down depending on the demand. In AWS, the Elastic Load Balancer distributes incoming application traffic across multiple EC2 instances for improved scalability and fault tolerance. AWS Auto Scaling can adjust the number of EC2 instances in response to traffic patterns, ensuring enough capacity to meet current demand. This entails setting a minimum and maximum number of instances and defining the scaling policies.

2. **Load balancing**: A load balancer accepts incoming network and application traffic and distributes it across multiple targets, such as EC2 instances, containers, and IP addresses, in multiple Availability Zones. This increases the availability and fault tolerance of the applications.

3. **Microservices architecture**: A monolithic application can be broken down into smaller, loosely coupled services, or microservices, each handling a specific business function. Each microservice can then be scaled independently, which enhances system scalability.

4. **Sharding**: This involves splitting a large database into smaller, more manageable parts, or shards, each holding a portion of the data. Sharding can significantly improve database performance and make it more scalable because requests can be processed in parallel across multiple shards.

5. **Caching**: Using services like Amazon ElastiCache to temporarily store (cache) copies of data that's in high demand can reduce the load on your databases and improve application performance, making it more scalable.

6. **Using serverless technologies**: With serverless technologies like AWS Lambda, you don't need to manage servers. Instead, your application can run and scale as needed, and you only pay for the compute power you use.

When we scale up (increasing the number of processors used), it helps to be mindful of Amdahl's Law to understand the gap between practical and ideal scaling.

There aren't specific graphs or charts to show these concepts, as each system's scalability measures are usually unique and depend on factors like application architecture and workload characteristics. Nevertheless, diagrams for AWS services like load balancer, EC2 instances and their distribution of traffic could be effective.

How can system reliability be improved?

Improving system reliability involves various strategies which include system backup, redundancy, automatic failover, fault tolerance, high availability, etc.

1. **System Backups**: Taking regular backups of data is crucial to manage potentially catastrophic scenarios. Database services such as Amazon RDS supports automatic backups of database instances. Backed-up data is encrypted on the server that hosts the DB instance and is encrypted during storage. AWS follows an incremental backup approach which means only the changes to the data since the last backup are saved.

2. **Redundancy**: Redundancy involves the duplication of critical components or functions of a system to increase its reliability. AWS offers redundancy though services like Amazon S3 which automatically replicates data across multiple systems in diverse geographical locations. Furthermore, with Amazon S3's versioning capabilities, you can preserve, retrieve, and restore every version of every object in your Amazon S3 bucket. This allows you to recover from both unintended user actions and application failures.

3. **Automatic Failover**: Automatic failover involves moving the operations from the primary location to backup locations without human intervention when an error occurs. A good example is AWS RDS Multi-AZ deployments which automatically failover to a standby database during maintenance, or failure, or when the Availability Zone is unusable.

4. **Fault Tolerance**: Fault tolerance prevents system-wide fail-

ures in the case of a component failure. AWS EC2 instances can
be designed to "heal" themselves i.e, when an instance becomes unhealthy, it is automatically replaced maintaining the desired capacity
and automation.

5. **High availability**: High availability involves building a system
that continues to operate effectively even when certain components
fail. AWS suggests implementing a multi-Availability Zone architecture for critical workloads to achieve high availability. Load balancing
across multiple Amazon EC2 instances in multiple Availability Zones
can ensure reliable and consistent performance.

A typical architecture diagram to represent the above-mentioned concepts might look like this:

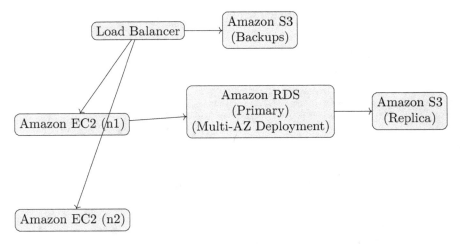

The interplay of these methods will be determined by the specific
requirements of each system, including its intended use, performance
needs, budget, and the potential impact of system downtime.

Remember, improving reliability comes with increased complexity
and cost. Hence, the choices should be made judiciously to balance
reliability and cost.

What measures can be taken to enhance system security?

Security is a pivotal point when designing, implementing, and maintaining cloud software architecture. For AWS Cloud users, there are several measures to enhance system security:

1. **Authentication and Access Control**: Only authenticated and authorized users should have access to data and resources. AWS provides IAM (Identity and Access Management) service for this purpose. With IAM, you can create users, groups, and roles to which you can grant permissions. IAM also enables federated user access, allowing you to use external identity providers to manage AWS resources.

For instance, IAM policies can look like this:

```
{
    "Version": "2012-10-17",
    "Statement": [
        {
            "Effect": "Allow",
            "Action": "s3:ListBucket",
            "Resource": "arn:aws:s3:::example\_bucket"
        }
    ]
}
```

This policy allows the holder to list items in 'example_bucket' on Amazon S3.

2. **Encryption**: Data should always be encrypted, both at rest and in transit. AWS provides tools like KMS (Key Management Service), S3 server-side and client-side encryption methods, SSL/TLS protocols for API endpoints, and VPN connections for encrypting in-flight data.

To illustrate, you might use KMS to manage cryptographic keys:

```
aws kms create-key --description "Example key for S3 encryption"
```

3. **Monitoring and Logging**: Always monitor and log your system's activities. Services like CloudTrail, CloudWatch, GuardDuty can help identify unusual behavior or unauthorized access attempts. They provide reports, graphs, alerts, or even enact automatic remedies via AWS Lambda functions.

4. **Firewall and Network Infrastructure**: Employing the tools AWS provides for maintaining a secure network infrastructure is crucial. These tools include Security Groups, Network Access Control Lists (ACLs), and AWS WAF (Web Application Firewall) for API Gateway or Load Balancers.

5. **System Updates and Patching**: Regularly update and patch your system to mitigate vulnerabilities. AWS Systems Manager 'Patch Manager' automates the process of patching managed instances.

6. **AWS Best Practices and Compliance**: AWS has a well-documented set of best practice guidelines for security. Following these can significantly improve your system's security. Also, ensure to set up your cloud environment in compliance with industry standards like PCI DSS, HIPAA, GDPR, etc.

7. **Incident Response**: Have an incident response process in place. Services like Amazon Macie help in identifying and protecting sensitive data.

8. **Security in Code**: Employ tools like AWS CodeStar to ensure security is embedded during the code build process. It's also important to conduct regular code reviews and onboard developers with best coding practices.

For more detailed information, it's advised to reference AWS Well-Architected Framework's Security Pillar whitepaper.

How do you ensure the maintainability of a system over time?

Maintainability of a cloud-based software system is the extent to which a system can evolve over time to continue to meet its requirements, both functionally and non-functionally. This primarily includes correcting faults and improving performance or other attributes. It also includes adapting the system due to changes in the environment.

Maintaining a system over time involves several integral components:

1. **Design Modularity:** A well-structured system is divided into independent modules or services. This follows the microservices architectural style and allows individual components to be maintained or upgraded independently without impacting the overall system. This is often used in AWS-based architectures and is helpful for teams working on various parts of the system.

2. **Automated Testing:** Test automation ensures that regression bugs are quickly identified, and any new changes do not break existing components. AWS CodePipeline and AWS CodeBuild offer CI/CD capabilities. DevOps practices, especially the test-driven development (TDD) approach guarantees that the codebase remains maintainable over time.

3. **Documentation:** Comprehensive documentation of your architecture, APIs, and services is crucial for maintainability. AWS provides several in-built tools for documenting your services like AWS CloudFormation Template Schema, which documents how AWS services are defined within an infrastructure.

4. **Infrastructure as Code (IaC):** IaC represents a shift in managing infrastructure, where infrastructure configuration is written into code and treated the same way as application software. Using AWS, you can define your resources via AWS CloudFormation or Terraform and version control your infrastructure the same way you do application code.

5. **Continuous monitoring and logging:** Regular system monitoring through AWS CloudWatch or AWS X-Ray, helps detect any anomalies early and fix them before they become significant issues. Additionally, it also aids in post-mortem analysis and prevents recurrence of past faults.

6. **Load management:** AWS provides services such as ELB (Elastic Load Balancer) and Auto Scaling to ensure the system is scalable and reliable. The smooth functioning of these services over time contributes to the maintainability of the system.

7. **Up-to-date dependencies:** It's essential to keep dependencies up-to-date to ensure the system's maintainability. AWS provides Dependabot, a tool that checks your dependencies and opens automated pull requests for any outdated ones.

Maintaining a cloud system, in sum, requires not only the anticipation of future requirements but also the ability to reflect these requirements in the design, programming, and execution of the system. The concepts and tools provided by AWS significantly assist in this process.

Can you discuss some strategies for load balancing in a highly scalable system?

Load balancing is a critical component in any scalable system, and AWS provides comprehensive services to ensure efficient load distribution across your resources.

1. **Elastic Load Balancer (ELB)**: It is a load balancing service for AWS deployments. ELB auto-scales your resources and distributes incoming application or network traffic across multiple targets, such as Amazon EC2 instances, containers, and IP addresses, in multiple Availability Zones. ELB can handle volatile workloads and scales your load balancer as traffic changes over time. It can automatically scale to the vast majority of workloads.

ELB supports the following types of load balancers: Application Load Balancers, Network Load Balancers, and Classic Load Balancers.

2. **Auto Scaling**: Auto Scaling in AWS helps you ensure that you have the correct number of Amazon EC2 instances available to handle the load for your application. AWS Auto Scaling monitors your applications and automatically adjusts capacity to maintain steady, predictable performance at the lowest possible cost.

There are several strategies to implement load balancing using these AWS services:

1. **Round Robin**: It's a simple method for distributing client requests across a group of servers. When a request comes in, the load balancer forwards the request to the next server in the list. The algorithm then moves that server to the end of the list.

2. **Least Connections**: This is a dynamic load balancing method. The load balancer forwards a request to the server with the least current connections to clients. The relative computing capacity of each server is factored into determining which one has the least connections.

3. **IP Hash**: The IP address of the client is used to determine which server receives the request. This method ensures that a client will always connect to the same server, assuming no servers are added or removed.

4. **Health checks**: Regular health checks to participating servers ensure that requests only go to servers that are available to process them. If a server fails to health check, it is taken out of the rotation until it passes a health check again.

5. **Session Persistence/Sticky Sessions**: In some cases (for example an e-commerce site where a user's shopping cart needs to persist), it's beneficial for a client to reconnect to the same server. This is handled using a persistent session where every request from a client always goes to the same server.

Here's the representation of a Load Balancer working with an Auto Scaling in AWS:

```
Client --request--> ELB --distribute request--> EC2 Instances
                     |
             AutoScalingGroup
```

Where ELB distributes incoming requests to multiple EC2 Instances tracked by an AutoScaling Group.

Remember, balancing load effectively and efficiently could save a significant amount of costs for a cloud-centric company. Smart strategies and good understanding of your own architecture and workload are key to maximize the benefits.

To further delve into formulas and graphs, you might need to dive into deep technical specifics of implementing above methods, balancing strategies, and network theories which might be a complex topic to be covered here.

How can redundancy improve system reliability?

System reliability is a crucial aspect of system design, especially in cloud computing environments such as AWS. Redundancy is one of the strategies that can be used to enhance system reliability.

Redundancy essentially means keeping additional or duplicate components, operations, or systems as a backup in case the primary ones fail. These components can be anything - from servers, databases, storage systems, to network links, etc. Redundancy is classified in different ways - hardware redundancy, software redundancy, and information redundancy.

Redundancy improves system reliability in the following ways:

1. **Reduction in System Downtime**: Redundant components ensure that the system keeps running even if a primary component fails.

For instance, imagine a system where you have deployed two identical databases (DB1 and DB2). If DB1 fails, DB2 can take over immediately, ensuring that the total system downtime is minimized.

2. **Quick Recovery from Failures**: Redundant systems can speed up a system's recovery from failures. With redundant components in place, the system can seamlessly switch operations from a failing component to a working one. This quick recovery can minimize the disruption to users.

3. **Increased System Lifespan**: Components of a redundant system can work in a rotating manner to prevent any single component from becoming overloaded. This can potentially increase the system's lifespan by reducing undue strain on any single component.

4. **Enhanced Data Protection**: Data redundancies, like using replication or backup schemes, can protect crucial data by storing it in multiple locations or forms. This can prevent data loss in case of any data-related mishaps.

To view redundancy's impact on system reliability in a more quantitative manner, we might use the concept of Mean Time Between Failure (MTBF) for components and Systems. MBTF is usually expressed in Hours.

MTBF of a component = Total operational hours / Number of Failures

If a single system without redundancy has a MTBF of 'X' hours, a redundant system (considering two components for simplicity) with the same components will technically double the MTBF (almost, not considering possible correlated failures), resulting in '2X' hours. Thus, the system's reliability is improved.

Overall, Redundancy aids in ensuring system scalability, reliability, security, and maintainability. It provides a safety net for system components and ensures seamless service to users even when unprecedented failures occur. AWS provides various services and features to implement redundancy, improving the reliability and resilience of systems deployed in its cloud environment.

Please note that excessive redundancy can lead to increased costs and complexity. Therefore, a balance is essential in designing redundant components for any system to manage cost-effectiveness and efficiency.

Please note that while redundancy can greatly enhance reliability, it should be one part of a comprehensive approach that includes things like regular system monitoring and updates, security protocols, maintenance processes, and disaster recovery planning.

How does encryption enhance system security?

Encryption plays a critical role in enhancing the security of systems, especially those using cloud-based services like AWS. It involves translating data into a secret code that only someone with the correct decryption key can read. This process helps protect sensitive information as it passes over the internet or is stored in databases, making it unreadable to unauthorized users. In AWS, encryption adds an extra layer of protection against data breaches and unauthorized access.

1. **Data At Rest:** AWS offers a range of encryption solutions for data at rest, including Amazon S3 Server-Side encryption (SSE) where each object is encrypted with a unique key, and as an additional safeguard, it encrypts the key itself with a master key that it regularly rotates. There's also AWS Key Management Service (KMS) for centralized control over cryptographic keys, helping you meet compliance requirements.

Example: Let's say a user wants to store documents in an S3 bucket. They can enable Server-Side encryption to ensure that data is encrypted before it's written to the disk. If an unauthorized person gains access to the S3 bucket, they won't be able to read the data without the unique key.

2. **Data In Transit:** Data being transferred between services or

over the internet is vulnerable to interceptions. AWS employs SS-L/TLS for securing network communications and establishing the identity of websites over the Internet. AWS services like AWS Certificate Manager provides easy SSL/TLS certificate management, and AWS Site-to-Site VPN creates secure, private connections between your remote network and your Amazon VPCs.

3. **Data Integrity:** Encryption also ensures data integrity by confirming that the data sent is the data received—without unintentional alterations or malicious tampering. Amazon Macie is a security service that uses machine learning to automatically discover, classify, and protect sensitive data such as Personally Identifiable Information (PII). AWS CloudTrail provides event history of your AWS account activity, including actions taken through the AWS Management Console, AWS SDKs, command line tools, and other AWS services.

For instance, consider a scenario where a user is sending confidential files from their local machine to an EC2 instance. They can use Secure Shell (SSH) protocol which employs public key encryption to eliminate risks of data being modified or intercepted during transfer.

```
Given data D and Encryption Key K, the encryption function might be written as:
E(D, K) = D'
where D' is the encrypted data or ciphertext.

The corresponding decryption function might be written as:
D(D', K) = D
where D is the plaintext.

Data in Transit might be represented as:
Secure Connection = E(Data, SSL/TLS Key)

The encryption function using the AWS KMS can be represented as:
SecureObject = E(D, E(K, MasterKey))
where MasterKey is the master encryption key from AWS KMS.
```

Please note that these are simplified examples of the encryption process and don't represent the actual complexity of encryption algorithms.

In summary, encryption is a crucial element in a comprehensive approach to security in the cloud. It acts as a security measure to keep confidential data away from unauthorized access. AWS offers built-in encryption features, making it easier for users to secure their data at rest and in-transit without requiring any changes to their applications or workflows.

How can code quality measures and refactoring improve system maintainability?

Code quality measures and refactoring help to improve system maintainability through several means. For instance, they provide a standard on how code should be written and organized, which in turn, streamlines the code base reducing the time and effort needed to understand and make modifications to the code. They help to identify and get rid of redundant and extraneous code, which decreases the chance of bugs occurring and makes debugging easier. They also provide emphasis on modularity, which creates a compartmentalized system that's less tangle-prone and easier to handle.

Here's a more detailed elaboration:

1. Improving Readability and Understandability: Enhancing code quality, primarily by writing clear, concise, and well-documented code, can make the software more maintainable. For instance, regulations might specify the use of meaningful name conventions and reasonably detailed commenting of code alongside clean and tidy formatting. All these measures boost readability and understandability, which means that developers will need less time to comprehend and edit the code later. This also enhances the speed at which new team members become productive.

2. Reducing Code Complexity: Refactoring plays a major role in reducing code complexity. It streamlines the code by eliminating unused variables, unnecessary statements, and duplicate code, thereby mitigating the chances of errors. Low complexity code is easier to maintain since it has fewer bugs and errors compared with intricate, complicated code.

For instance, suppose we have a function $f(x)$ where x is the complexity of the original code, and $f(x)$ represents the number of bugs you might expect as a result. A high complexity x will yield a higher bug potential $f(x)$, making it harder to maintain the code. On the other hand, refactoring to reduce complexity leads to a smaller x, reducing bug potential $f(x)$ and hence enhancing maintainability.

3. Enabling Modularity: Code quality measures often emphasize modularity. This means, the codebase is divided into independent modules or components, each responsible for a specific functionality. When any changes or updates are to be made, developers know immediately where to look. This compartmentalization means developers can modify or fix issues on one module without impacting others, reducing interdependencies and ensuring easier and safer evolution of the software.

4. Utilizing Automated Testing: Automated testing (part of the refactoring process) helps ensure that changes made during the development process do not introduce new bugs or re-introduce old ones. This improves the reliability and maintainability of the software system since issues can be caught and fixed early and continuously.

5. Promoting Code Reuse: Code quality measures promote the reuse of code. By only needing to write and maintain the functionality once, this can significantly decrease development time and increase maintainability. For instance, if a bug is found within the reused code, only one fix is needed, and all occurrences of the reused code will be automatically updated.

In summary, good code quality measures and refactoring can improve system maintainability disproportionately. A lower learning curve due to increased readability, reduced code complexity, improved modularity, automated testing, and code reuse can significantly decrease the amount of time, effort, and cost needed for maintenance.

Can you give an example of a situation where you had to improve the scalability, reliability, security, or maintainability of a system?

Let's take an example of a web application that was initially built on a traditional environment with a single server, which hosts the web server and database on the same machine. As time passed, the application gained popularity, and traffic spiked. The system frequently went down, creating a great deal of frustration for the users along with losing potential business revenue.

To improve the scalability and reliability, the architecture can be migrated to AWS with the following services:

1. **Amazon EC2 (Elastic Compute Cloud)**: EC2 instances will be used to host application servers. Multiple instances can be created to distribute the traffic load. This will help in providing scalability.

2. **Amazon RDS (Relational Database Service)**: It is a managed service which makes it easy to set up, operate, and scale a relational database in the AWS cloud. It provides cost-efficient and resizable capacity while automating time-consuming administration tasks such as hardware provisioning, database setup, patching, and backups.

3. **Amazon ELB (Elastic Load Balancer)**: This will distribute the traffic among the multiple EC2 instances, ensuring no single machine is overwhelmed with too much traffic. ELB improves the scalability and reliability of the application.

4. **Amazon S3 (Simple Storage Service)**: For static content (image files, video files, etc.), S3 can be used. S3 provides secure, durable, and highly scalable object storage.

5. **Amazon CloudFront**: It is a content delivery network (CDN) which will cache the static content closer to the end users, thereby improving the site's speed and reducing the latency.

6. **Amazon Auto Scaling**: This is used to automatically adjust the number of EC2 instances in response to traffic patterns. When demand for EC2 instances increases, Auto Scaling automatically increases the EC2 instances count and reduces it when the demand decreases, leading to cost optimization and better performance.

Implementing these changes will significantly improve the scalability and reliability of the web application hosted in AWS. This is just one of the many ways AWS services can be leveraged to improve the scalability and reliability. Different combinations of services can be used based on the project requirements.

Please note that this is a simplified example. In a real-world scenario, there would be additional considerations. It's best to consult with an AWS Solutions Architect or a similar professional with experience in AWS infrastructure planning before making such changes.

How do these four factors (scalability, reliability, security, maintainability) interact with each other in system design?

Scalability, reliability, security, and maintainability are core components for designing and operating a system, especially in the cloud environment. These factors often intertwine with each other in a complex fashion where improving one might have repercussions on the others.

1. **Scalability and Reliability**: These two factors are often in direct correlation. When a system is designed to be scalable, it can handle an increase in load by adapting resource allocation dynamically. In turn, this often enhances the reliability of the system, as there are often backup resources that can take over if primary resources fail. In AWS, scalability can be ensured through services such as Elastic Load Balancing and Auto Scaling. Similarly, services like Amazon S3 provide data durability by automatically creating and storing copies of all S3 objects across multiple systems. Here, scalability increases reliability.

2. **Scalability and Security**: The relationship here can be complex. While designing a system to be more scalable, it may involve more instances, bigger networks, and more attack surfaces to be protected, therefore potentially reducing the security. On the other hand,

services like AWS Shield for DDoS mitigation, AWS IAM for Access Management, and AWS WAF for web application firewall can strengthen security, but requires careful planning and implementation and may reduce scalability if not handled well.

3. **Reliability and Security**: Good security design often boosts reliability by reducing the threat of attacks that can cause system or service unavailability. AWS provides various security services such as Amazon Inspector for assessing application security, Amazon Macie for data privacy, and Amazon GuardDuty for threat detection which enhances both security and also indirectly reliability.

4. **Maintainability and the rest**: Maintainability enables a system to undergo changes with a degree of ease. These changes could be modifications, updates, or corrections. The ease of maintainability often increases with stronger security, higher reliability, and better scalability. Being able to quickly and effectively respond to new security threats, increase resource allocation, or restore system operations are all indicators of high maintainability. AWS CloudFormation provides a simple way to create and manage a collection of related AWS resources, enabling provision and updating your resources in an orderly and predictable fashion which increases maintainability.

Here is an example of a graph that depicts these relationships qualitatively:

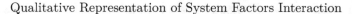

Qualitative Representation of System Factors Interaction

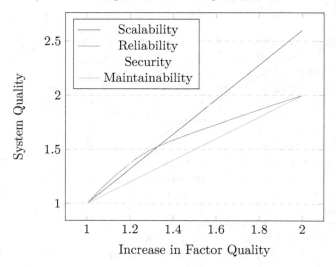

Increase in Factor Quality

In this graph, an increase in any one of the x-axis factors (e.g., Improved Scalability or Improved Security) leads to a qualitative improvement in overall system quality. However, the exact rate (slope) of improvement may differ depending upon the existing system configuration, implemented services, and specific factor interactions.

Therefore, in practice, these four factors require a balancely focused approach. Overemphasis on one factor without regarding the others might lead to an unoptimized system design. AWS provides a comprehensive selection of services, each designed with these factors in mind, to help create a balanced and optimized system design.

Chapter 3

Designing Scalable and Reliable Systems on AWS

This chapter embarks on a focused exploration of building systems on AWS that stand resiliently against demand fluctuations and unforeseen failures. It starts by laying out the foundational design principles for scalability, ensuring that systems can efficiently handle growth, whether anticipated or sudden. From understanding the basic tenets, we venture into the realm of reliability, emphasizing how AWS applications can be architected to guarantee consistent performance and availability. Embracing these principles, the chapter then transitions into patterns for resilience in AWS, offering readers a treasure trove of strategies and insights to ensure their AWS applications can recover and adapt from potential disruptions. Capping off the chapter, we delve into real-world best practices and use cases, providing readers with practical applications of these principles and an understanding of how businesses worldwide are leveraging AWS for scalable and reliable solutions.

3.1 Design Principles for Scalability

What is scalability and why is it important for a system?

Scalability is the capability of a system, network, or process to handle a growing amount of work, or its potential to be enlarged to accommodate that growth. In the context of AWS Cloud Software Architecture, it involves providing adequate computing resources such as storage, compute capacity, and database throughput to deliver expected levels of performance, reliability, and efficiency as your user base or workload increases.

Importance of Scalability:

Scalability is important for a variety of reasons:

1. **Manage Growth:** As your application grows, you'll need to handle larger amounts of data, more requests per second, and other increased demands. If your system isn't scalable, it can't accommodate this growth effectively.

2. **Resilience:** Scalable systems can better handle load spikes, because they can add resources to meet demand. This makes your application more robust and resilient.

3. **Cost**: Scalability allows you to manage costs more effectively. You can scale up or scale out based on demand, meaning you're only paying for the resources you need at any given time.

4. **Performance**: Maintaining performance at scale ensures a consistent user experience. Your system needs to respond just as quickly whether it's serving 1 user or 1 million.

Design Principle for Scalability on AWS

Designing for scalability on AWS often involves using the following principles:

1. **Microservices**: Break your application into smaller, loosely coupled, independently-deployable services. Each can scale independently.

2. **Serverless Architectures**: Serverless lets you run your code without provisioning or managing servers. AWS Lambda is an example. It scales your application based on the workload.

3. **Multi-Tier Architectures**: Spread out your load among different kinds of resources. This often involves using a mix of EC2 instances, database services like RDS or DynamoDB, and caching with services like ElastiCache.

4. **Horizontal Scaling(Scaling out/in):** Rather than upgrading the resources of an individual component (Scaling up/down), it involves increasing the number of components. In AWS, you can achieve this by increasing the number of EC2 instances to handle more requests.

Example: Consider a web application hosted on an Amazon EC2 instance. Initially, the app could handle the load with a single EC2 instance. As the user base grows, the demands increase. Instead of using a larger EC2 instance (scale-up), you could distribute the load across multiple EC2 instances (scale-out) to handle the growth.

To graph scalability, you might plot the number of requests per second (RPS) a system can handle against the number of servers. Optimally scalable systems would demonstrate a linear relationship, where doubling the number of servers doubles the RPS, for example.

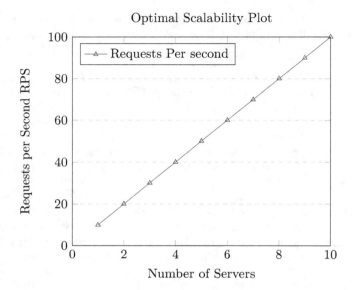

In the plot above, we can see a linear increase in the number of requests that can be handled as the number of servers increase.

How does AWS support system scalability?

AWS (Amazon Web Services) provides a broad set of products and services you can use as building blocks to run sophisticated and scalable applications. Running your applications in the AWS Cloud can help you move faster, operate more securely, and save substantial costs; all while benefiting from the scale and performance of the cloud.

When it comes to designing scalable systems, there are several key principles that AWS emphasizes:

1. **Design for Failure and Nothing Fails:** While AWS services are designed for high availability, infrequent infrastructure or service disruptions can still occur. Therefore, best practices for AWS architecture includes assuming that failure can and will occur, and

designing your systems to be resilient to these failures.

2. **Decouple Your Components:** Decoupling drives the agility of your system and improves the ability to evolve over time. With loosely coupled systems, you can develop, deploy, update, and scale most of the parts of your system independently.

3. **Use Multi-tier Architectures:** Multi-tier architectures are generally better because they provide a separation of concern. AWS offers services like EC2 (Elastic Compute Cloud) for compute layer, RDS (Relational Database Service) for database layer, and ELB (Elastic Load Balancing) for distributing incoming traffic across multiple EC2 instances.

4. **Distribute Your System to Replicate Data and Failure Handling:** The AWS Cloud spans 77 Availability Zones within 24 geographic regions around the world. By distributing your systems and data across these Availability Zones within a region, you can design your architectures to be robust against the failure of a single location.

Here's how AWS services support scalability:

1. **Auto Scaling:** Auto Scaling allows you to scale your Amazon EC2 capacity up or down automatically depending on criteria you define. With Auto Scaling, you can ensure that the number of Amazon EC2 instances you're using scales during demand spikes to maintain performance, and decreases automatically during demand lulls to minimize costs. This flexibility is key to ensuring you're only using (and paying for) the resources you need.

2. **Load Balancing:** Elastic Load Balancing automatically helps distribute incoming application traffic across multiple Amazon EC2 instances. It helps to ensure your application is fault tolerant and that you are making maximum use of your resources.

3. **Amazon RDS:** Amazon RDS is a managed relational database service that provides you with six familiar database engines to choose from, including Amazon Aurora, MySQL, MariaDB, Oracle, and SQL Server. You can use the AWS Management Console's point-and-click

interface to scale your database's compute and storage resources.

For a visual representation, consider a web application running on an EC2 instance. As traffic to your web application grows, you can meet increased demand by simply adding more EC2 instances behind a load balancer (ELB). If your database layer becomes a bottleneck, you can use Amazon RDS's scaling features to add read replicas or increase the instance size.

Please note that all these architectures are high-level designs, and you need to adapt them based on your specific use case. AWS offers various design patterns and architectural best practices to help you build highly scalable, flexible, secure, and cost-effective cloud architectures.

What are some AWS services that can help achieve scalability, and how do they work?

Scalability is the ability of a system to effectively manage increasing workloads with no degradation in performance, even under an expanding demand. AWS offers a myriad of services that help in building a scalable system.

1. **Amazon EC2 (Elastic Compute Cloud)** Amazon EC2 provides secure, scalable, on-demand compute capacity in the cloud. It is designed to make web-scale computing more accessible to developers. It provides you with complete control of your computing resources and lets you run on Amazon's proven computing environment.

How it works: You can quickly scale capacity, both up and down, as the computing requirements change. Vertical scaling can be accomplished in EC2 by changing the EC2 instance types. Horizontal scaling involves (usually automated) adding or removing EC2 instances from the environment based on demand.

2. **Amazon S3 (Simple Storage Service)** Amazon S3 is an object storage service that offers industry-leading scalability, data availability, security, and performance. It's great for backup and restore, data

archiving, and big data analytics.

How it works: Amazon S3 automatically scales to high request rates. For example, your application can achieve at least 3,500 put, copy, post, or list requests per second per prefix in a bucket. There is no limit to the amount of data you can store in an Amazon S3 bucket.

3. **Amazon RDS (Relational Database Service)** Amazon RDS makes it easy to set up, operate, and scale a relational database in the cloud.

How it works: With Amazon RDS, you can deploy multiple editions of scalable databases in minutes with cost-efficient and resizable hardware capacity. Amazon RDS manages the database administration tasks, so you don't have to.

4. **Elastic Load Balancing** ELB automatically distributes incoming application traffic across multiple targets, such as EC2 instances. It ensures that only healthy targets receive traffic by regularly checking the health of registered targets and automatically removing any that are unresponsive.

How it works: As the traffic to your application varies over time, Elastic Load Balancing scales your load balancer and updates the DNS entry. Note that the DNS entry also specifies the time-to-live (TTL) as 60 seconds, which ensures that the client's resolver gets updated IP addresses on subsequent requests.

5. **Amazon SQS (Simple Queue Service)** Amazon SQS allows you to decouple and scale microservices, distributed systems, and serverless applications. SQS eliminates the complexity and overhead associated with managing and operating message oriented middleware.

How it works: SQS makes it simple and cost-effective to send, store, and receive messages at any volume. There's no upfront cost, and you pay only for what you use. As the volume of messages increases, AWS automatically scales the message handling.

6. **AWS Auto Scaling** AWS Auto Scaling monitors your appli-

cations to maintain steady, predictable performance at the lowest cost. It helps applications meet their performance and availability requirements, and maximizes cost effectiveness.

How it works: AWS Auto Scaling automatically adjusts capacity to maintain steady performance at the lowest possible cost. It uses Amazon CloudWatch to retrieve application's metrics, and then use this data to scale out/in as needed.

For example, here is an AWS Auto Scaling configure for an EC2 instance:

```
resource "aws_autoscaling_policy" "asg_up" {
  name                   = "asg_up"
  scaling_adjustment     = 2
  adjustment_type        = "ChangeInCapacity"
  cooldown               = 300
  autoscaling_group_name = aws_autoscaling_group.asg.name
}
```

It represents a policy that increases the capacity of the Auto Scaling group by two instances. The 'cooldown' parameter ensures that another scaling activity does not start until 300 seconds after the completion of previous activity.

Note: These are not the only services AWS provides for scalability, it also includes DynamoDB, EFS, SNS, and more.

How does auto-scaling work in AWS and how would you set it up?

Auto-scaling in AWS works by dynamically adjusting the number of EC2 (Elastic Compute Cloud) instances in response to varying workloads or demands. In essence, you can set conditions for when to increase (scale out) or reduce (scale in) the number of instances using AWS CloudWatch and auto-scaling rules.

As instances are added or removed based on these rules, AWS handles the distribution of incoming application traffic across these instances by incorporating a load balancer.

Setting up auto-scaling involves the following steps:

1. **Launch Configuration:** The first step is creating a launch configuration. This involves specifying the AMI id (Amazon Machine Image), instance type, Key Pair, and any roles that the instance needs. Here is how you can do it in the AWS Management Console.

2. **Auto-Scaling Group:** Once you have the launch configuration, you create an auto-scaling group. You define how many instances you want to start with, your VPC and subnets, and select your launch configuration.

Auto-Scaling Policy: This is where you define the conditions under which auto-scaling happens. You can create a Scale Out policy (to increase instances) and a Scale In policy (to decrease instances). These policies are triggered based on CloudWatch alarms.

Let's say your EC2 instance's CPU utilization goes beyond 70%, and you've set a scale-out policy to launch 1 more instance for this situation. As soon as CloudWatch identifies that the CPU utilization has crossed the 70% threshold, it triggers the auto-scaling policy, and 1 more instance is added to your auto-scaling group.

On the other hand, suppose during off-peak hours the CPU utilization drops below 20%. If you've set a scale-in policy for this scenario, CloudWatch triggers this policy when the threshold is crossed, and removes 1 instance from your group.

Below is a diagram that illustrates this:

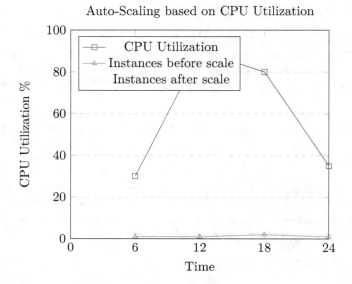

The blue line in the chart represents the CPU utilization changing with time. The red markers (triangle) represent the number of instances before the scale event happens. The green markers (circle) represent the number of instances after the autoscaling rules are applied.

This is a basic example and in reality, there can be many other factors to consider when setting up auto-scaling such as predictable load changes, configuring a cool-down period, health check-ups, and more.

Final notes on costs: AWS charges for auto-scaling policies per instance-hour consumed for instances launched, so the cost of running auto-scalable architecture can depend on your application's load patterns and your defined scaling policies.

Can you describe horizontal scaling and vertical scaling and give examples where each might be appropriate?

To begin, both horizontal scaling and vertical scaling are methods to increase capacity and manage the growth of an application, but they approach this in different ways.

Horizontal Scaling (also known as scale-out): This involves adding more nodes (server systems) to the existing pool to distribute the workload more evenly between them, essentially increasing the breadth of your system.

Vertical Scaling (also known as scale-up): This involves increasing the power of individual nodes such as adding more powerful CPUs, increasing the amount of RAM, or adding more storage.

The basic representation of Horizontal and Vertical Scaling would look like this:

Horizontal Scaling	Vertical Scaling		
Node 1			
Node 2	CPU	RAM	Storage
Node 3	:	:	:
:	CPU	RAM	Storage
Node n			

Where would you use each one?

1. Use Horizontal Scaling when:

- Your application's resource demands are variable or dynamic.

- You want to enhance redundancy in your system, thus making it more failproof.

- Useful when you need to handle heavy incoming network traffic.

- In cases when you're using Microservices, Docker containers, or any serverless architecture.

For example, if you have an e-commerce site that experiences variable levels of traffic throughout the day, scaling horizontally allows you to handle peak traffic loads efficiently.

2. Use Vertical Scaling when:

- Your application needs more computing power than currently available.

- You deal with applications that depend on the execution of single-threaded processes.

- More suitable for applications requiring access to local resources.

For example: A database server might benefit from vertical scaling because they typically use single-threaded processes and would benefit from faster CPUs and more memory.

Remember that in the context of AWS and cloud-based solutions, scaling horizontally is typically a more viable option as you cannot truly max out your resources due to the virtually unlimited capacity of the cloud. It also promotes distributed system design which is good for fault isolation and redundancy.

How can you use Elastic Load Balancing to help with scalability?

Elastic Load Balancing (ELB) is an AWS service that automatically distributes incoming application traffic across multiple targets, such as Amazon EC2 instances, containers, and IP addresses, in multiple Availability Zones. ELB helps to achieve better fault tolerance in your applications by seamlessly providing the load balancing capacity that is needed in response to incoming application traffic.

In terms of scalability, ELB allows you to handle varying traffic levels. By distributing traffic across multiple resources, ELB ensures that no individual resource becomes a bottleneck, thus maintaining the responsiveness of your applications. When the demand increases, new resources can be automatically added and ELB will distribute the traffic among all available resources, not just the ones that were initially set up.

For example, suppose you have an application running on two EC2 instances and you decide to auto-scale your application by adding two more instances because the number of requests is increasing. After the new instances are ready, ELB automatically starts to distribute incoming requests among all four instances.

You can also design your system to scale out (add more instances) or in (remove instances) automatically with EC2 Auto Scaling and ELB. EC2 Auto Scaling will automatically add more instances if CPU utilization is above a specific threshold, and remove instances if CPU utilization is below a certain threshold. This way, you can maintain a consistent user experience during both peak and off-peak hours.

However, in practice, it's slightly more complex because new instances need time to boot and configure, and there can be variations in the number of requests each instance receives. Therefore, you'll need to monitor and adjust your thresholds to ensure that you have enough capacity to handle the load, but not too much to waste resources.

Furthermore, ELB scales itself automatically based on the demand, handling varying volumes of traffic incoming to your environment. AWS does this by adjusting the resources of the load balancer and doing the necessary health checks to make sure your environment's capacity meets your follower set's demand. This ensures the optimal routing mechanism for your application or website.

To sum up, by properly configuring your ELB and EC2 Auto Scaling settings, you can build a highly scalable system on AWS that can handle varying levels of traffic efficiently and cost-effectively.

How do the concepts of stateless and stateful impact scalability?

Stateless and stateful are concepts that play a highly significant role in designing scalable systems.

Stateful Applications:

Stateful applications store data about each client session and use this information for all requests from that session. This implies that all requests from a particular session needs to be processed by the same server where session state is stored. This complicates scalability since adding new servers does not help much due to session affinity requirements.

For example, consider a stateful server that currently serves 1000 customers and is at its maximum capacity. When a new server is added, the existing customer sessions cannot be moved or shared between the old and new server since they are stateful. The new server can only serve new customers, thus not truly aiding scalability.

Stateless Applications:

Stateless applications, however, do not store any data regarding client sessions. Each request is processed based on the information that comes with it and there's no need to know the prior interaction details.

This makes stateless applications highly scalable as any server can process any incoming request. The load balancer can distribute the requests evenly among all the available servers without considering any session information.

To give an example, imagine the previous scenario with a stateless server instead of a stateful one. When a new server is added, the load balancer can start directing some of the requests to it immediately. This allows the system to handle more customers, demonstrating improved scalability.

In conclusion, stateless applications are much more scalable than stateful applications due to their ability to distribute requests evenly across multiple servers. Still, stateful applications may be necessary for certain use-cases where session data needs to be preserved. In those situations, other strategies such as sticky sessions, distributed cache/state, or database storage may need to be considered for improving scalability.

What factors should be considered when planning for future scalability of a system on AWS?

Planning for future scalability of a system on AWS involves considering several factors. Here are the main ones:

1. **Decoupling**: Break up your system into independent components to reduce the interdependencies and allow each component to scale separately. AWS provides several services such as AWS SQS (Simple Queue Service) for decoupling layers or components in your system. A decoupled system design can enable your application to be more reliable and operationally efficient, and it can improve fault isolation and service levels.

2. **Serverless Architectural Patterns**: Serverless patterns mean deploying your services without thinking about server management. Services like AWS Lambda can execute your code in response to events and automatically manage the resources for you. It scales with incoming traffic.

3. **Databases (Denormalization, Indexing, Partitioning)**: AWS has a variety of database technologies available (like Amazon DynamoDB for NoSQL, Amazon RDS for relational databases, Amazon Redshift for OLAP) which can help in scaling the data layer of your application. You can use denormalization to reduce the need for complex joins in queries. Indexing can speed up data retrieval times. Sharding or partitioning the data can distribute the load and make scaling easier.

4. **Caching**: Increasing scalabilty can also include using caching systems such as Amazon ElastiCache. Caching frequently accessed data can reduce latency and offload work from your databases.

5. **Content Distribution Network (CDN)**: AWS offers CDN service through CloudFront. CDN stores cached copies of content, such as videos or images, closer to the end users, which can increase the speed of delivery and reduce the load on your backend servers.

6. **Auto-Scaling**: Auto-scaling is a key feature provided by AWS where resources are automatically added or removed depending on the load of your application. Elastic Load Balancing, EC2 Auto Scaling, Amazon Aurora Auto-Scaling, and AWS Fargate are some of the auto-scaling services.

7. **Statelessness**: Making your applications stateless, where each request can be treated as an independent transaction, makes it easier to scale out your application. If needed, manage session state outside the application, for example, into a database service such as Amazon DynamoDB.

8. **Monitoring and Automation**: AWS CloudWatch can be used to monitor your application and system performance, and set alarms for when certain thresholds are crossed. This aids in automatic scaling as mentioned above. AWS Auto Scaling enables this automated capacity management.

Here's a high level example of how you might structure an auto-scaling, decoupled system:

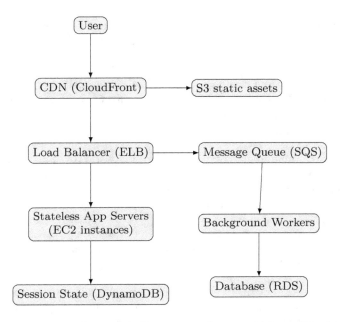

Each arrow '<—>' indicates a point at which scaling (either manual or automatic) can occur. The specific scaling planning would depend on detailed load, traffic, and performance profiling of the application.

Each point where a service is listed (e.g., 'CDN (CloudFront)', 'Load Balancer (ELB)', etc.) represents a point where a different AWS service plays a role in the system's scalability.

Can you provide an example of a real-life project where you had to design for scalability on AWS?

Suppose we are working on an e-commerce web service that is expected to serve hundreds of thousands of users around peak shopping times such as Black Friday. The core requirements include handling a large volume of read and write requests and delivering data with minimal latency.

The first principle of designing for scalability is to adopt a stateless architecture. Therefore, we decouple our web application into multiple tiers: a web tier and a data tier.

1. **Web tier**: Here the user requests are initially landed. For this, we would leverage Amazon EC2 (Elastic Compute Cloud) instances behind an Elastic Load Balancer (ELB), which can automatically distribute incoming application traffic across multiple EC2 instances.

2. **Data tier**: It handles storing and retrieving of data. For this, we would use Amazon's managed database service RDS (Relational Database Service) and store static content such as images in Amazon S3 (Simple Storage Service) to deliver data with minimal latency.

To ensure scalable read capacity, we can take advantage of 'Read Replicas' in RDS, which help you scale out beyond the capacity constraints of a single DB instance for read-heavy database workloads.

However, we must also consider aspects like network latencies, the load balancer distributing traffic unevenly due to sudden spikes in requests, session stickiness, and varying data retrieval times.

In terms of an architectural diagram, here is an extremely simplified version of our architecture:

```
User requests
    ↓
Elastic Load Balancer (ELB)
    ↓
EC2 Instances
    ↓
RDS DB Instances --- Read Replicas (if necessary)
    ↓
Amazon S3
```

Of course, the architectural decisions must be made considering the specific use-case requirements, cost efficiency, security, and regional availability among others. Also, there are other services such as DynamoDB (for non-relational databases), AWS Auto-Scaling Services (to automate the scalability and ensure cost-effectiveness), etc. which we can integrate based on specific use-case requirements. Additionally, for designing a reliable system, we would need to consider incorporating services for backup, restoring, and disaster recovery tasks.

The process of designing for scalability often involves iterative testing and modifying system architecture to meet specific performance goals. Truly, it's an ongoing endeavor as we refine our systems to meet evolving customer needs and leverage advancements in technology.

How would you manage the trade-off between scalability and cost-efficiency in AWS?

Managing the trade-off between scalability and cost-efficiency in AWS involves careful design choices, capacity planning, and monitoring usage trends. Here are some strategies to balance cost and scalability:

1. **Auto Scaling Groups**: A primary way to handle scalability in a cost-effective way is by using AWS Auto Scaling Groups (ASG). ASGs allow for systems to scale out and in based on defined policies such as CPU utilization or network traffic. For example, you could set a policy to scale out when CPU utilization is beyond 70% and scale in when it's less than 40%. This way you only pay for instances when they're actually needed to handle the load.

2. **Spot Instances**: AWS offers spare Amazon EC2 computing capacity, or spot instances, at up to 90% off the On-Demand price. If you have applications that have flexible start and end times, Spot Instances can offer significant cost savings.

3. **Over-provision CPU and Memory**: By over-provisioning CPU and memory, you can handle sporadic traffic spikes without needing to scale. This can also reduce costs because you avoid the time and resources required to scale.

4. **Reserve Capacity in Advance**: For predictable workloads, you can purchase reserved instances to achieve significant savings when compared to on-demand pricing.

5. **Use a CDN (Content Distribution Network)**: Using a CDN such as Amazon CloudFront can significantly reduce the load on your services and hence, the number of instances you need to run.

The cost function of AWS services can be modelled as follows:

```
Cost = f(instance_type, instance_hours, Network_IO, storage_size, data_out)
```

For example, the cost associated with an EC2 instance can be modelled as:

```
Cost = Hourly_Rate * Instance_Hours
```

The optimal cost can be found by minimizing the cost function subjected to meeting your application's performance requirement (e.g. response time, throughput).

It's also important to remember that cost and scalability are not always directly correlated. For example, by refactoring an application to do more with less (more efficient algorithms, better caching, etc), you might be able to actually reduce costs and improve scalability at the same time.

At the end, to effectively manage the trade-off between scalability and cost-efficiency, continuous monitoring, once again, plays a very important role. Tools like Amazon CloudWatch and AWS Trusted Advisor can give insights into the resource usage, opportunity to save costs, and much more.

3.2   Building Reliability into AWS Applications

How would you define reliability in the context of AWS applications?

Reliability in the context of AWS applications can be defined as the ability of an application to perform its required functions under stated conditions for a specific period of time. It involves two key aspects:

1) The application should recover from infrastructure or service disruptions without manual intervention or, at most, with minimal human efforts. This implies that the system should be designed in such a way that it can handle unexpected faults and be resilient enough to recover from them. Fault tolerance measures such as backups, replication, and redundancy are often used to achieve this.

2) The application should dynamically acquire computing resources to meet demand and mitigate disruptions. This speaks to the scalability and elasticity of the application, which ensure that the application can respond to changes in load without sacrificing performance or availability.

In AWS, several services and mechanisms help to build reliability into applications. These include:

- **AWS Auto Scaling**: This service adjusts capacity to maintain steady, predictable performance at the lowest possible cost.

- **Amazon Simple Queue Service (SQS)**: It is a fully managed message queuing service that enables you to decouple and scale microservices, distributed systems, and serverless applications.

- **AWS Elastic Beanstalk**: This service provides an easy-to-use service for deploying and scaling web applications and services developed with Java, .NET, PHP, Node.js, Python, Ruby, Go, and Docker on familiar servers such as Apache, Nginx, and IIS.

The reliability of an AWS application can be measured by its uptime and its ability to recover from disruptions, both of which can be represented by the following formula:

$$Reliability = \frac{TotalTime - Downtime}{TotalTime}$$

Where:

- Total Time refers to the total period under consideration.

- Downtime refers to the total time during which the system was not available or not operating correctly.

A system that is 100% reliable would be available and operating correctly for the entire Total Time period. However, achieving 100% reliability can be unrealistic or cost-prohibitive in many situations due to the nature of hardware failures, network outages, and other unforeseen events. Because of this, many organizations aim for "five nines" (99.999%) reliability, which permits a downtime of about five minutes per year.

As such, the goal for an architect designing AWS applications should be to strike a balance between achieving a high degree of reliability and the costs (in terms of resources, time, and money) necessary to achieve that reliability.

Lastly, it is important to note that reliability is not a static attribute — it can change as system load varies, maintenance is performed, updates are rolled out, etc. Therefore, it is crucial to monitor system reliability continually, using services like Amazon CloudWatch to detect and respond to any declines in reliability promptly. AWS also recommends conducting regular game days, where potential failure scenarios are rehearsed to ensure the system can recover from failures efficiently and effectively.

How does AWS support system reliability?

AWS supports system reliability through a combination of resiliency and redundancy, utilizing a multi-tier infrastructure of Regions, Availability Zones, data centers, and edge locations.

1. Regions and Availability Zones:

AWS has several regions worldwide, each consisting of multiple availability zones (AZs). AZs within a region are spatially separated, powered by distinct power sources, and connected via redundant, ultra-low-latency networks. This design ensures that system components are not affected by the same issues simultaneously.

2. AWS CloudFormation:

AWS also provides a system known as AWS CloudFormation that allows for replication of resources across multiple regions and AZs, enabling automated recovery from any single point of failure.

3. Load Balancing:

AWS Elastic Load Balancing automatically distributes incoming application traffic across multiple targets such as EC2 instances, containers, and IP addresses in multiple AZs. This makes it able to handle the varying load of your application traffic in a single or multiple AZ.

4. Auto Scaling:

With AWS Auto Scaling, it's easy to ensure that you are utilizing the right resources in the right quantities to handle the demand on your application. Auto Scaling takes care of scaling out to make sure that your application maintains steady, predictable performance even when demand grows, and scaling in when demand subsides to help you reduce costs.

5. Data Replication:

AWS supports several types of data replication, including synchronous and asynchronous replication. Synchronous replication helps to ensure consistency across all replicas by waiting for all replicas to acknowledge receipt of a write before the write is considered successful. Asynchronous replication does not wait for all replicas to acknowledge receipt before considering the write successful. It is useful when low latency is more important than immediate consistency.

6. Snapshot and Backup:

AWS provides tools such as AWS Backup and Amazon EBS snapshots to take point-in-time backups, ensuring data resilience.

AWS also implements mechanisms to handle disruptions and automate recovery, with solutions for setup, scaling, monitoring and maintenance. One needs to properly configure such features to achieve high reliability.

To quantify reliability, you can use metrics such as:

- Availability, which can be measured as the ratio of system uptime to total time.

$$Availability = \frac{Uptime}{TotalTime}$$

- Durability, which can be measured as the probability that data will not be lost over a given period.

$$Durability = 1 - \frac{\text{Number of data units lost}}{\text{Total number of data units}}$$

AWS provides CloudWatch and CloudTrail, services to monitor these metrics and set alarms if they drift from defined thresholds.

For example, if the availability of a critical database drops below 99.9% (the threshold), an alarm will notify the system administrator.

The ways in which AWS supports system reliability are too numerous to fit into this text, but I hope this provides a good overview. It shows that AWS has multiple built-in constructs to support high system reliability if properly utilized. However, the onus still falls on the system designers to create a reliable architecture with these AWS services.

What are some strategies for improving the reliability of an AWS application?

Improving the reliability of an AWS application involves implementing several key strategies that take advantage of the robust set of tools and features provided by AWS. Here are some major strategies:

1. **Automation:** AWS provides automation tools such as AWS CloudFormation and Elastic Beanstalk which allow you to automate many tasks thereby reducing human errors. Wherever possible, automate time-consuming, manual tasks.

2. **Fault Isolation (Cell-based Architecture):** A cell-based architecture, also known as a sharding pattern, divides the overall application into different microservices or modules wherein each cell/module can operate independently even if the other cells/modules fail.

3. **Distributed Systems Best Practices:** Implementing distributed systems best practices such as idempotency, exponential back-offs, and jitter can help improve application reliability. For instance, idempotency ensures that a function can be run any number of times and produce the same result, which can prove beneficial in handling network issues.

4. **Graceful Degradation:** This strategy consists of building applications that can continue to function and provide service, even if some parts of the system fail. For example, if a recommendation engine fails, the application can degrade to a state where it shows popular items instead of personalized recommendations.

5. **Monitoring and Review:** Detect and identify issues in the application using CloudWatch, AWS X-Ray, and Trusted Advisor.

6. **Testing:** Regularly load test and stress test your applications with tools like AWS Fault Injection Simulator. This helps evaluate the application's behavior and limitations in a controlled environment.

7. **Backup and Restore Strategy:** Implement a backup strategy that meets Recovery Time Objective (RTO) and Recovery Point Objective (RPO) of your application using services like AWS Backup.

To appreciate how these function, we can consider an example of a service that uses AWS CloudFormation for automation, cell-based architecture for fault isolation, and AWS X-Ray for monitoring. Here's a rough representation of how such a system might look like:

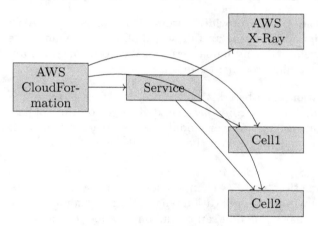

In this graph, we depict an AWS CloudFormation that deploys a service and multiple cells. It incorporates automation, fault isolation, and consistent monitoring to improve reliability. The service communicates with the individual cells (incorporating a cell-based architecture), and its operations are monitored by AWS X-Ray.

Remember - improving reliability is a continuous process. Regularly monitor your systems, seek feedback, learn from incidents, and evolve your practices to maintain and improve your application's reliability.

For more detailed explanation on these strategies and additional techniques on how to improve AWS application reliability, refer to the AWS Well-Architected Framework's Reliability Pillar whitepaper.

How can you use AWS services like Amazon S3 or AWS Glacier to improve data reliability?

Amazon S3 and AWS Glacier are both highly durable, secure storage services offered by AWS. They can greatly improve the reliability of your data in several ways:

1. **Durability and Redundancy:** Both S3 and Glacier are designed to deliver 99.999999999% (11 9's) durability. This is achieved through data replication across multiple geographically separated data centers. Effectively, this ensures the survival of your data even in the event of a total data center failure.

2. **Data Versioning:** S3 supports versioning, which allows you to preserve, retrieve, and restore every version of every object in your bucket. This makes it possible to recover from both unintended user actions and system failures.

3. **Lifecycle Management:** With S3's lifecycle management policies, you can instruct S3 to automatically migrate data to cheaper storage classes like S3-IA (Infrequent Access) or AWS Glacier for long-term archiving.

4. **Encrypted Data:** Both S3 and Glacier offer server-side encryption with multiple options for key management. Depending on the sensitivity of your data, you can choose to manage your own keys or to let AWS manage them for you.

5. **Consistency Model:** Amazon S3 provides strong read-after-write consistency for PUTS and DELETES of objects. This means that once a write occurs, any subsequent read request will return the

most recent data.

For example, consider a data pipeline that ingests and processes data, storing the resultant data into an Amazon S3 bucket. If this pipeline fails at any point, the data written up to that point remains intact in S3. The pipeline can be restarted from the point of failure without any data loss, thereby increasing the overall reliability of the application.

Configuring a lifecycle policy to automatically migrate objects from S3 standard to S3-IA after 30 days and then to Glacier after 90 days might look like this:

```
{
  "Rules": [
    {
      "ID": "Move␣to␣S3-IA␣after␣30␣days",
      "Prefix": "",
      "Status": "Enabled",
      "Transitions": [
        {
          "Date": "30␣days",
          "StorageClass": "STANDARD_IA"
        },
        {
          "Date": "90␣days",
          "StorageClass": "GLACIER"
        }
      ]
    }
  ]
}
```

In the context of the AWS Well-Architected Framework, using services like Amazon S3 and AWS Glacier helps to meet the reliability pillar's design principles of "Test recovery procedures", "Automatically recover from failure" and "Scale horizontally to increase aggregate system availability".

How does replication work in AWS and how can it contribute to system reliability?

Replication is a critical factor in building reliable Amazon Web Services (AWS) applications. Essentially, replication involves creating multiple copies of data and services across different geographic regions or availability zones. AWS offers numerous services to facilitate replication, such as Amazon RDS (Relational Database Service) for database replication, Amazon S3 (Simple Storage Service) for data replication, and AWS Route 53 for DNS (Domain Name System) routing.

Let's consider the example of Amazon RDS:

Amazon RDS has a feature called Multi-AZ deployments that helps to increase data reliability and reduce failover times. This feature automatically provisions and maintains a "standby" copy of your database in a different Availability Zone. Any changes to the "primary" database (like data insertion, updates, or deletions) are automatically replicated on the standby database using synchronous data replication. When a planned or unplanned outage of the primary DB instance occurs, Amazon RDS performs an automatic failover to the standby, ensuring that data read and write operations can continue with minimal interruption.

As a cloud architect, it is also important to be aware of the CAP theorem regarding distributed data storage systems. CAP theorem states that it's impossible to simultaneously guarantee Consistency, Availability, and Partition Tolerance. Therefore, a careful balance should be maintained considering your application's requirements.

In essence, the additional replicas created through replication mitigate the risk of data loss and increase system availability, thus helping ensure the reliability of AWS applications. The following diagram illustrates the concept:

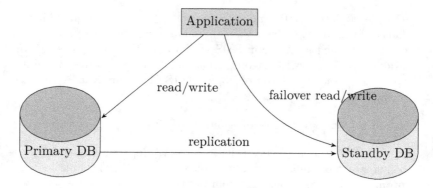

The similar capability also exists with Amazon S3 where Cross-region replication (CRR) can be set up to copy objects across Amazon S3 buckets in different AWS regions synchronously. This is especially useful in reducing latency times when users access data from various geographic locations.

In conclusion, using replication in your AWS architectures can greatly enhance the reliability of your system by providing real-time redundancy for your data and services, and enabling your applications to be highly available.

How can monitoring and alerting tools like AWS CloudWatch contribute to reliability?

AWS CloudWatch is a monitoring and management service designed for developers, system operators, site reliability engineers (SRE), and IT managers. It provides data and insights that can be used to monitor applications, understand and respond to system-wide performance changes, optimize resource utilization, and get a unified view of operational health.

CloudWatch plays a critical role in building reliability into AWS applications in the following ways:

1. **Monitoring:** CloudWatch continuously observes your AWS en-

vironment to gather and store operational data. This includes metrics, such as CPU usage, memory usage, and network traffic; logs, or detailed records of application operations; and events, or changes in your AWS resources.

2. **Alerting:** With CloudWatch alarms, you can monitor any CloudWatch metric over time, whether default or custom, and receive notifications when the metric breaches a threshold you set. Alarms can trigger actions, such as sending a notification through Amazon Simple Notification Service (SNS), auto-scaling your resources, or initiating system changes through AWS Lambda functions.

3. **Analytics:** By accessing CloudWatch insights and dashboards, you can analyze, visualize, and gain insights from your operational data. This helps in identifying patterns, anomalies, and trends that might impact reliability.

4. **Automation:** Through event-driven computing, CloudWatch can respond to state changes to your AWS resources. For example, if a server fails a health check, CloudWatch can automatically reboot the server, enhancing reliability without manual intervention.

In terms of reliability, these capabilities enable proactive measures such as predictive maintenance, anomaly detection, and system failure prevention.

For example, consider an AWS-based web application. If the average CPU usage on its EC2 instances suddenly spikes, this could lead to a performance degradation or even cause the application to crash. However, with CloudWatch, you'd have the resource usage being tracked over time. An alarm can be set to trigger when the CPU usage gets too high, and this could be used to initiate auto-scaling, adding more instances to handle the increased workload and hence maintaining a reliable application.

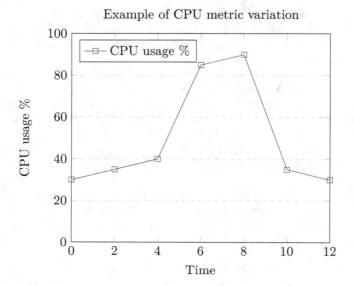

This chart visualizes a spike in CPU usage (at time 6-8), which should trigger an CloudWatch alarm for taking corrective actions, contributing to the reliability of the system.

What is the concept of fault tolerance, and how is it achieved in AWS?

Fault tolerance is a crucial aspect of system design that allows a system to continue running smoothly and to deliver seamless service, even in the event of a partial system failure. Fault-tolerant design ensures that your system doesn't have a single point of failure, and it has redundancies put in place to compensate for possible system component failures.

With AWS applications, fault tolerance can be achieved through distributing instances across multiple locations, such as different regions or availability zones that are insulated from failures in other zones.

Services like Amazon RDS (Relational Database Service), Amazon S3 (Simple Storage Service), and Elastic Load Balancing automatically replicate data across different zones to ensure high availability and durability.

AWS best practices include:

1. **Using Multiple Availability Zones**: Each AWS region is composed of multiple distinct locations known as Availability Zones (AZs). Deploying instances in multiple AZs provides a higher level of availability and fault tolerance.

- For example, AWS' RDS Multi-AZ deployments provide enhanced availability and durability by automatically replicating database updates between two AZs.

2. **Auto Scaling**: This feature lets you maintain application availability and lets you scale Amazon EC2 (Elastic Compute Cloud) capacity up or down automatically according to specified conditions.

- For example, if an Amazon EC2 instance in one AZ becomes unreachable due to a fault, Amazon EC2 Auto Scaling can detect the fault and replace the instance, keeping your application available and your users happy.

3. **Elastic Load Balancing**: Elastic Load Balancing (ELB) automatically distributes incoming application traffic across multiple targets like Amazon EC2 instances. With support for the detection of unhealthy instances within an AZ, ELB can reroute traffic to healthy instances until the unhealthy instances have been restored.

4. **Amazon S3 for data replication**: Amazon S3 provides 99.999999999% durability for objects stored in the service by replicating data across at least three geographically separate zones within an AWS region.

Please note that these strategies will increase fault tolerance, but also the cost. As such, it's important to undertake a thorough analysis of risks vs costs when engineering your systems for fault tolerance in

AWS.

Can you provide an example of a real-life project where you had to improve the reliability of an AWS application?

Let's consider an online e-commerce store as an example. When it started, it was serving a small customer base using simple AWS instances where front-end, back-end, and database were residing on the same server. However, as the business grows, the need for a more reliable, robust, and scalable system becomes important.

1. **Break Monolith into Microservices:** It's typical to split the monolithic system into several microservices, for example, Users, Orders, Inventory, and so forth. Each component needs independent scaling, and through this approach, it minimizes the blast radius - the capability of one faulty component that would bring the whole system down.

2. **Multi-AZ Deployment:** To make the system more reliable, deploying the application in multiple Availability Zones (AZs) is recommended. Amazon RDS service allows you to run your database instances in multiple AZs, which enhances the database's fault tolerance.

3. **Auto-scaling and Load Balancing:** Load balancers distribute incoming application or network traffic across multiple targets, such as EC2 instances. Amazon EC2 Auto Scaling ensures that the system has the optimal number of EC2 instances to handle the load. An unexpected increase or decrease in traffic won't render the system less reliable.

4. **Redundancy:** Redundancy minimizes the impact of a single point of failure. For example, keeping multiple copies of data in S3 and using Multi-AZ feature of Amazon RDS provide redundancy and reliability.

5. **Disaster Recovery:** Regular backups for data stored in databases are necessary. Also, employing version control strategies for the production code and infrastructure setup aids in quick recovery in case of failure. AWS provides several tools such as AWS Backup and AWS CodeCommit for these purposes.

Remember, reliability means the system should recover from infrastructure or service disruptions, dynamically acquire resources to meet demand, and mitigate disruptions such as misconfigurations or transient network issues. All these improvements help when building reliability into AWS applications.

How do you balance the need for reliability with cost considerations on AWS?

Achieving the right balance between cost and reliability for AWS applications essentially involves making some trade-offs based on your business goals and application requirements. Here's an outline of strategies you can use:

1. **Design for Failover**: Make use of services that offer built-in redundancy and failover capability, reducing the need to provision and pay for extra, stand-by resources. For instance, Amazon RDS provides automatic failover support by maintaining a standby in a different Availability Zone. While this incurs some cost, it eliminates the need for manual intervention and reduces downtime, thus potentially saving costs that could occur due to loss of business during downtime.

2. **Auto Scaling**: With AWS Auto Scaling, you can ensure that you have the correct number of EC2 instances available to handle your application load. You can scale out to improve reliability during peak demand and scale in during periods of low demand to reduce costs. You're only paying for what you use, and you're ensuring high availability.

3. **Lifecycle Management and Scheduling**: Use lifecycle man-

agement features of AWS services to transition your data between different storage classes based on access patterns, which will optimize cost and availability. Also, you can schedule stop/start instances for non-production workloads (like shutting down development instances over the weekend) to reduce costs.

4. **Reserve Instances for Predictable Workloads**: For databases or applications with predictable demand, you can reserve instances to save cost over On-Demand pricing. The cost-effective nature of Reserved Instances, coupled with its guaranteed availability, contributes to the reliability factor.

5. **Use Spot Instances for Interruptible Workloads**: Spot instances can handle interrupts and save up to 90% compared to On-Demand pricing. However, they have no reliability guarantees and can result in data loss if not properly managed.

6. **Cost-optimized Architectures**: Deploy multi-tier application architecture patterns on AWS: break application into microservices and deploy them in Containers or Serverless services. This results in flexible scaling and reduces costs.

7. **Monitoring, Alerting and Automating Response**: Use CloudWatch and AWS Lambda to automate responses to system anomalies. It can proactively enable failover, backup and recovery actions, reducing potential downtime costs.

8. **Cost Explorer & Budgets** : AWS Cost Explorer helps to visualize and manage AWS costs and usage over time, enabling you to identify trends, detect cost overruns, and forecast for future. AWS Budgets let you set custom cost and usage budgets that alert you when the thresholds you've set are exceeded, ensuring the balance between cost and reliability.

Thus, you can continuously optimize costs through analysis and automated adjustment to application architecture in AWS. The goal is cost optimization without compromising reliability. Balancing these parameters should be a continuous process during the lifetime of the application, and AWS provides a variety of tools to help achieve this.

For a visual graph or diagram, one could consider a scatter plot with cost on one axis and reliability on the other. As you move towards higher reliability, the cost also gradually increases. The optimal point is where the increase in reliability and the corresponding increase in cost reach a balance, and that would be adapted based on individual business needs.

How does AWS help in ensuring the reliability of a system in the case of region-specific issues?

AWS offers a number of ways to ensure the reliability of a system, even in the case of region-specific issues. These methods center on the concepts of availability zones and multi-region replication.

1. **Availability Zones (AZs):** AWS resources are housed in highly secure facilities in different geographic locations, known as regions. Each AWS region is composed of multiple isolated and physically separate locations within that geographic area, called Availability Zones (AZs). Each AZ is engineered to be isolated from failures in other AZs, and to provide inexpensive, low-latency network connectivity to other AZs within the same region. Deploying your applications across multiple AZs can help you protect your applications and data from the failure of a single location and improve their ability to remain operational, even in the face of unforeseen issues.

2. **Multi-region replication:** AWS services such as Amazon S3, Amazon RDS, and AWS DynamoDB support cross-region replication. This feature allows a copy of your data to be stored and updated in more than one region, providing an additional safety net in case of region-specific problems. If there is an issue affecting one region, applications can failover (switch) to the duplicate system in a different, unaffected region.

Here is an example of how AWS's multi-region replication works with Amazon S3. Suppose you have an S3 bucket in the US East (N. Virginia) region and set up replication to a bucket in the EU (Ireland) region. Once setup is complete, whenever an object is put into the source bucket, AWS automatically replicates it to the destination bucket in the other region.

3. **Using Route 53 for DNS failover:** Amazon Route 53 is a highly available and scalable Domain Name System (DNS) web service that is designed to direct users to the right endpoint for your application. Route 53 can respond intelligently to regional disruptions by routing traffic to healthy resources.

For example, you can configure Route 53 to check the health of your resources, such as web servers. If it finds that a server is unavailable, or that a whole region is experiencing issues, Route 53 can automatically route traffic to a healthy resource in a different region.

In summary, AWS provides mechanisms to ensure system reliability even in the face of region-specific issues. The platform's architecture allows for geographic distribution of resources and supports replication of resources across multiple regions. AWS's Route 53 service can also intelligently reroute traffic in response to regional disruptions.

3.3   Patterns for Resilience in AWS

What are some common patterns for resilience in AWS?

Resilience in AWS is achieved by a combination of a variety of patterns that address and handle common failures. Here are some of the most used patterns for resilience in AWS:

1. **Redundancy and Replication:** This is one of the most fundamental patterns for resilience. It involves creating multiple copies of data or multiple instances of services across different regions or availability zones. This ensures that even if one region or zone experiences a failure, the services continue to operate seamlessly. AWS provides

solutions such as Amazon S3 for storage redundancy and Amazon RDS for database redundancy with Multi-AZ deployments.

2. **Auto Scaling & Load Balancing:** Auto Scaling allows services to automatically scale up or down based on the demand, reducing the risk of service disruption due to sudden traffic spikes. AWS Auto Scaling combined with Elastic Load Balancing distributes incoming application traffic across multiple targets, such as EC2 instances.

3. **Failover Mechanism:** In case of a failure, a failover mechanism smoothly switches from the primary component to a standby component. AWS RDS Multi-AZ deployments and Route 53 DNS service are excellent examples of these.

4. **Graceful Degradation:** This pattern allows the system to continue functioning but provide a reduced level of functionality when one or more of its components fail. This can be achieved using methods such as AWS Lambda functions with a Dead-Letter Queue (DLQ).

5. **Rate limiting and Throttling:** By limiting the rate at which requests are processed, AWS services can provide protection against resource exhaustion. API Gateway is a good example of a service offering rate limiting.

6. **Circuit Breaker:** The circuit breaker pattern helps to prevent a network or a service from being repeatedly hit with requests that it cannot handle. This can prevent a single failing component from bringing down the entire system - an example of the pattern in AWS is to use a service like AWS Step Functions to handle state transitions and error handling in a serverless application.

7. **Sharding:** This divides a database into smaller more manageable parts, also known as database shards. Each shard contains the same schema but different data. If you're using Amazon Aurora for example, you can divide your databases into smaller databases.

8. **Queuing:** Queueing requests and processing them one by one can prevent the system from becoming overwhelmed. AWS provides

a service called Amazon SQS which offers scalable and secure queuing services.

Remember, these patterns are not an exhaustive list and these can be combined in numerous ways to achieve a more resilient system. The key is to understand the nature of your service and its requirements to choose the appropriate combination. Also, it's important to adopt a fail-fast mentality, where systems quickly shut down components that are causing problems, and replace or bypass them to minimize overall impact.

How can multi-AZ deployments improve the resilience of an AWS application?

Multi-AZ (Availability Zone) deployments significantly improve the resilience of an AWS application by minimizing the impact of single points of failure and increasing its availability and uptime. It allows for continuous operation, even if some part of the infrastructure fails or experiences an outage. Amazon's availability zones (AZs) are physically separated within a typical geographical area (region), and they have independent power, cooling, and networking to insulate applications from the failure of a single location.

The following are some of the ways multi-AZ deployments contribute to resilience:

1. **Fault Isolation:** Each AZ is a standalone facility with its power source, network connectivity, and cooling system. If one AZ experiences a problem, the others remain unaffected. This fault isolation prevents failures from spreading between zones.

2. **Data Replication:** Services like Amazon Relational Database Service (RDS) and Amazon Elastic Block Store (EBS) provide automatic data replication across AZs. This means that even if one AZ goes down, the database remains available and the application can still function using data in the other zones.

3. **Traffic Distribution:** Services like Amazon Elastic Load Balancer (ELB) and Amazon Route 53 can distribute traffic evenly across multiple AZs, thereby ensuring that no single zone becomes a bottleneck. If one AZ becomes unhealthy or goes down, these services can automatically reroute the traffic to the remaining healthy zones.

4. **Disaster Recovery and Backup:** Multi-AZ deployment can be used as part of a disaster recovery plan. Data and services backed up in multiple AZs can be quickly restored in case of any disaster or catastrophic failure.

Overall, by leveraging multi-AZ deployments in AWS, one can significantly improve the resilience and availability of their cloud-based applications and services, ensuring consistent performance and virtually uninterrupted service availability. However, the costs, data transfer speed (latency), and application complexity can increase with the number of AZs used, so a careful cost-benefit analysis is necessary when deciding the number of AZs to use for a resilient system.

How does the concept of loose coupling contribute to resilience in AWS?

Loose coupling is a design principle at the core of distributed and scalable systems. It governs the manner in which components within these systems interact with each other. In loosely coupled architectures, each component is independent and has little to no knowledge of the definitions of other separate components.

By using loose coupling in AWS architecture, you can create a system that is resilient and less likely to fail, because a failure in one component does not directly impact others. The features of AWS services are designed to support building loosely coupled systems and to add redundancy to prevent single points of failure.

Let's look at some ways loose coupling contributes to resilience in AWS:

- **Failure isolation**: Loose coupling ensures that one component's failure doesn't affect the others. If a component does go down, the others can continue functioning independently. This significantly mitigates the risk of the entire system failing due to a single component's failure.

- **Scalability**: In a loosely coupled system, individual components can be scaled to handle higher loads without having to scale the entire system. This makes it easier to manage system load in a cost-effective manner. For example, in AWS you can scale EC2 instances independently from RDS databases according to their own requirements.

- **Flexibility and Agility**: Because components in a loosely coupled system are independent, it becomes easier to update or replace a component without affecting the rest of the system. This gives you the ability to rapidly adapt to changing business needs or to introduce new technologies.

Here are a few AWS architecture principles that support loose coupling:

1. **Using Elastic Load Balancing (ELB) and Amazon Route 53**: You can distribute traffic across multiple EC2 instances in a Region or route traffic to multiple resources or regions to increase the availability of your application.

2. **Implementing Amazon Simple Queue Service (SQS) or Amazon SNS (Simple Notification Service)**: SQS lets you decouple and scale microservices, distributed systems, and serverless applications, and SNS enables you to send messages or notifications directly to users or other distributed services.

3. **Taking advantage of AWS Lambda**: It allows you to run code without provisioning or managing servers, which helps in creating loosely coupled system components.

Here is a text representation of loosely coupled architecture:

```
                    +--------+
                    |  User  |
                    +----+---+
                         |
                         v
              +--------+-------+
              | Route 53 / ELB |
              +--------+-------+
                  /          \
                 v            v
            +----+---+    +---+----+
            |  EC2   |    |  EC2   |
            +----+---+    +---+----+
                 |            |
                 v            v
            +----+---+    +---+----+
            |  RDS   |    |  RDS   |
            +--------+    +--------+
```

In this diagram, we see that each instance of EC2 is independent of the others, as is each instance of RDS. This is the fundamental concept of loose coupling, and when it comes to AWS, it provides resilience by ensuring failures are isolated, resources can be scaled independently and system components are easier to manage.

Can you discuss some techniques for handling partial failures in an AWS application?

Resilience is a critical aspect of Cloud Architecture. To create robust systems on AWS, we need to design with fault-tolerance in mind. Here are some techniques for handling partial failures in an AWS application:

1. **Retry with Exponential Backoff and Jitter**: Handling transient failures is crucial to improving the resiliency of the application. Implementing a retry strategy helps to rerun the failed requests. AWS SDK provides a default configuration for retries, and also provides an option to customize the strategy. The Exponential Backoff algorithm

attempts retries but gradually elongates the waiting time because repeated retries may cause resource throttling. Adding Jitter mixes some randomness in the delay to avoid multiple requests from flooding the server simultaneously.

2. **Circuit breaker design pattern**: This pattern allows a service to fail quickly, avoiding waiting for unresponsive services indefinitely and clogging resources. AWS SDK does not provide a built-in circuit breaker, but it can be implemented easily. Netflix's Hystrix library is a popular choice for this in the Java ecosystem.

3. **Consistent Hashing**: Partial failures can result in overloaded nodes when the load is not evenly distributed. AWS provides services like Elastic Load Balancer (ELB) to handle load distribution. Still, for some special requirements or to distribute load across multiple caches or databases, consistent hashing can be used to prevent imbalanced loads when a node goes down or comes up.

Consistent Hashing maps requests (keys) to a set of servers (values) in such a way that when a server is added or removed, only a small fraction of keys are remapped.

For example, suppose we have n cache machines, we can assign each cache machine a point on the edge of a circle, further take a key, hash it, and map it onto a point on the edge of the same circle. Then assign it to the first cache machine which is encountered going clockwise from the key's point. Thus, when a cache machine fails, the keys that were assigned to it are distributed evenly among the remaining caches.

4. **Task Execution and Coordination**: AWS provides services like SWF (Simple Workflow Services) and Step Function to handle such tasks. Amazon SQS (Simple Queue Service) can also be used to create a decoupled, fault-tolerant architecture.

5. **Auto-scaling and Load balancing**: AWS provides auto-scaling functionality to handle the dynamic load and prevent single point of failure. In case a server goes down, auto-scaling adds a new node to maintain the desired capacity. Load balancers distribute the incoming requests to multiple nodes to prevent any one node from becoming a

choke point.

6. **Redundancy**: AWS provides options to launch resources in multiple locations (Like multiple Availability Zones). This way, if one zone goes down, your application will still be running in another zone.

In summary, there is no one-fits-all solution, and it's all about finding the right balance for your particular case. Therefore, AWS provides a vast range of tools and strategies to handle these failures and they are well-documented, so you can always find the one that suits your application the best.

How can services like AWS Lambda contribute to resilience in AWS?

AWS Lambda is a compute service that lets you run code without provisioning or managing servers, essentially enabling a serverless architecture. AWS Lambda contributes to the resilience of the architecture in several ways:

1. **Auto-scaling**: Lambda functions scale automatically, executing in parallel to precisely match the size of your workload. With AWS Lambda, you can process an arbitrary number of simultaneous requests, thereby providing high availability.

For example, let's say your code needs to process 1000 requests per second. AWS Lambda can scale automatically from zero to 1000 invocations per second without any intervention from you.

2. **Fault tolerance and self-healing**: AWS Lambda is designed for fault tolerance, with built-in redundancy and automatic retries. Functions are independently deployed and executed, meaning a single function failure will not cause system-wide failure.

The AWS Lambda service is also self-healing; it automatically replaces failed compute resources and maintains function availability.

3. **Event-driven processing**: AWS Lambda can respond automatically to system events such as changes to data in an S3 bucket or a change in system state. This means that it can automatically recover from failures that would otherwise require manual intervention, improving system resilience.

4. **Reduced operational complexity**: By managing your server resources, AWS Lambda helps reduce the complexity of your operations, making it easier to ensure high availability and disaster recovery.

5. **Microservices architecture**: AWS Lambda supports the microservices architecture pattern, where applications are divided into small, loosely coupled services. This can increase resilience by limiting the potential impact of any one service's failure on the overall system.

The following diagram illustrates how AWS Lambda contributes to a resilient architecture:

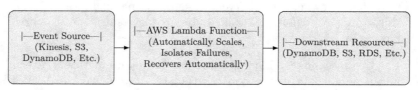

Let's take an example of redundancy and automatic retries in AWS Lambda.

If you have configured an AWS Lambda function to read changes in a Kinesis stream, Lambda service automatically creates enough instances of your function to handle the incoming event rate. If any of these instances fail, Lambda service will automatically retry the failed batch of records until processing succeeds or the data expires. Thus providing the resilience in case of failure.

How can Amazon DynamoDB be used in patterns for resilience?

Amazon DynamoDB is a managed NoSQL database service provided by AWS that is known for its durability and resilience. It can be used in patterns for resilience in several ways, for example by leveraging its built-in features such as on-demand capacity, automatic scaling, and global tables to ensure high-availability and fault-tolerance.

1. **On-demand Capacity**: DynamoDB allows you to switch between provisioned and on-demand capacity mode. In the provisioned capacity mode, you specify the number of read and write capacity units that you expect your application to require. However, in on-demand capacity mode, DynamoDB flexibly adapts to the traffic patterns of your application, providing capacity exactly when it's needed, contributing to resilience by accommodating unexpected traffic surges and preventing throttling.

2. **Auto-scaling**: DynamoDB's auto-scaling feature can be used as a pattern for resilience. Auto-scaling uses Amazon CloudWatch metrics to analyze utilization. You set target utilization percentages for read and write capacity, and auto-scaling adjusts provisioned capacity up or down, as needed within minimums and maximums you define, allowing you to meet performance requirements and keep costs down.

3. **Global Tables**: DynamoDB global tables provide a fully-managed solution for multi-region read and write data access, thereby adding resilience against regional failures. During normal operations, global tables in different regions automatically are kept in sync. If one region becomes unresponsive, your application can failover to another region.

4. **Point-in-time Recovery (PITR)**: DynamoDB provides built-in support for point-in-time recovery, which can protect your tables from accidental write or delete operations. With point-in-time recovery, you can restore any backup data to new tables.

5. **DAX (DynamoDB Accelerator)**: DynamoDB Accelerator (DAX) is a fully managed, in-memory cache that can reduce Amazon DynamoDB response times from milliseconds to microseconds, even at millions of requests per second. This helps ensure that your application can maintain high performance and drive resilience during traffic spikes.

6. **DynamoDB Streams**: This feature captures table activity, and it can be used for real-time analytics, replication, and trigger-event driven scenarios.

Therefore, DynamoDB, with its fast, flexible, and reliable features and functions, is instrumental in implementing resilience and maintaining the steady-state operation of an application in AWS cloud computing.

How can you improve resilience by using multiple AWS services together (e.g., Elastic Load Balancer with Auto Scaling)?

One way of improving resilience in AWS is by combining multiple AWS services like Elastic Load Balancer (ELB) and Auto Scaling together. By using these services in conjunction, you can efficiently handle incoming traffic and maintain high availability even when experiencing high levels of load, thereby preventing any single point of failure.

Elastic Load Balancer (ELB)

Amazon ELB automatically distributes incoming application traffic across multiple targets, such as Amazon EC2 instances. It achieves this by constantly monitoring the health of the registered instances and routing traffic only to healthy instances. It enhances the fault tolerance of your applications as unhealthy instances are not utilized, thus providing robustness.

Auto Scaling

AWS Auto Scaling monitors your applications and automatically adjusts capacity to maintain steady, predictable performance at the lowest possible cost. Auto Scaling enables you to follow the demand curve for your applications closely, scaling capacity up or down automatically according to conditions defined for workload.

Using ELB with Auto Scaling

Using both simultaneously, ELB would distribute the incoming traffic to the instances and Auto Scaling would ensure that the quantity of instances is adequate to handle the level of application load.

Some advantages of this integrated implementation:

1. **Increased Availability**: ELB distributes traffic only to healthy instances. If an instance fails, Auto Scaling will automatically replace it maintaining the desired capacity.

2. **Fault Tolerant**: It prevents any single point of failure as ELB distributes traffic to multiple instances and in case of failure, Auto Scaling replaces them.

3. **Cost-Effective**: With Auto Scaling, you don't have to provision and pay for resources that sit idle.

For example, let's consider a web application with the following setup:

- Uses an ELB to balance the load between multiple EC2 instances.

- The EC2 instances are part of an Auto Scaling group set to maintain 2-6 instances based on CPU usage. The CPU threshold triggers are set on lower than 30% for scale in and higher than 70% for scale out.

In idle state with low traffic, Auto Scaling maintains the minimum number of instances (e.g., 2). As traffic to your web application increases, the CPU usage of those instances also increases. Once the CPU usage hits 70%, Auto Scaling recognises this and launches new instances. Now ELB sees these new healthy instances and starts to distribute incoming traffic among more instances. This way we maintain a good user experience even in peak usage times.

On the other hand, when the load decreases and the CPU usage drops below the 30% threshold, Auto Scaling also starts reducing the number of instances. ELB will stop directing traffic to those instances that Auto Scaling is terminating.

This is the combination of ELB and Auto Scaling in action, providing resilience, availability and cost-effectiveness to your applications.

How does AWS support resilience in terms of data backup and recovery?

AWS provides multiple tools and services for data backup and recovery to support resilience. These include AWS Backup, Amazon S3, and Amazon Glacier. Besides these, AWS also facilitates taking snapshots of data volumes and launching them when needed. The tools in AWS support data backup and recovery on both an immediate and scheduled basis. Here we will discuss the specific mechanism each of these tools provides to support resilience.

1. **AWS Backup** - AWS Backup is a unified, fully managed backup service that simplifies the process of backing up data across AWS services. It allows users to centrally manage and automate the process of backing up data across AWS services in the cloud and on premises. This enhances overall systems resilience by enabling prompt recovery in case of any disaster that could compromise data integrity. You can customize backup policies and retention times based on business requirements, thus ensuring high availability and resilience.

2. **Amazon S3** - Amazon S3 (Simple Storage Service) is an object storage service that provides scalability, data availability, security, and performance. This means customers of all sizes and industries can use it to store and protect their data for a range of use cases. The versioning feature in S3 allows multiple variants of an object to be kept in the bucket. The existing versions of the file can be quickly fetched and deployed when needed, which greatly enhances systems resilience.

3. **Amazon Glacier** - Amazon Glacier, now known as Amazon S3 Glacier, is a low-cost cloud storage service for data with longer retrieval times. It is designed to be very durable, and it is suitable for long-term backup and data archiving. Data can be recovered either in bulk or on an as-needed basis, thus enhancing resilience by ensuring business continuity even in cases of extensive system failure.

4.Card**EBS Snapshots** - EBS (Elastic Block Store) snapshots are a point-in-time copy of your data. It is a backup that's taken at a specific point in time. The EBS Snapshot can be used to enable disaster recovery, migrate data across regions or accounts, improve backup compliance, and/or mitigate and protect against ransomware and disasters. A copy of the disk can be saved to an S3 bucket from where this can be called to create a new EBS volume.

Moreover, AWS supports automation of the backup processes using AWS Lambda, which can provide additional resilience by reducing the chance of human error and ensuring that backing up data is not overlooked or neglected.

To achieve high resilience and data protection, it's also essential to follow the 3-2-1 rule:

- Three copies of data: in production, local backup, and offsite/remote backup.

- Two different media types: such as an SSD, HDD, or cloud storage.

- One copy offsite: to ensure data safety during a disaster.

To illustrate, if these backup and recovery tools were nodes on a graph where edges represented data flow, it may look like this:

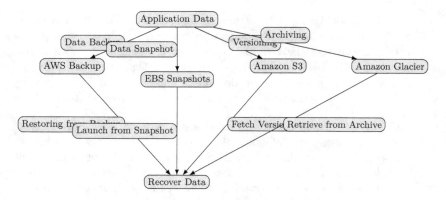

In this way, AWS provides various ways to backup and recover data for enhanced resilience of your applications and services hosted on AWS. As IT environments become more complex with data spread across various services, centralized and automated backup solutions are crucial for maintaining business continuity and achieve data resilience.

Can you provide an example of a real-life project where you implemented patterns for resilience in AWS?

Let's take a real-life project example of an e-commerce website where I implemented patterns for resilience. The website receives thousands of user requests concurrently and needs to have high availability and fault tolerance to manage heavy traffic and potential system failures.

Key services used in this project include Amazon EC2, Auto Scaling, Elastic Load Balancing, Amazon S3, Amazon RDS, and AWS Route 53.

1. EC2 Auto-Scaling: AWS Auto Scaling monitors the applications and automatically scales capacity to maintain steady, predictable performance. The resilience pattern here is to ensure that the number of EC2 instances scales up during heavy traffic (peak hours) and scales

down during low traffic.

2. Elastic Load Balancing (ELB): Using load balancing, incoming traffic gets distributed across multiple EC2 instances. This ensures a lower load on individual systems and enhances performance and redundancy. If one EC2 instance fails, the load balancer redirects traffic to the remaining running EC2 instances.

3. Multi-Availability Zones (Multi-AZ) AWS RDS: Enabled for the relational database used by the e-commerce site. This automatically creates and maintains a synchronous standby replica in a different Availability Zone. During DB instance failure, Amazon RDS performs automatic failover to the standby, offering high availability and failover support for database instances.

4. Route 53: For Domain Naming System (DNS) web service. It's designed to route end users to Internet applications on behalf of globally distributed and low-latency DNS.

5. Amazon S3: Used for backup and restore functionality. Automated backup scripts were written ensuring data is backed up to S3 at regular intervals. This serves as a contingency mechanism in case of data loss.

Here's a simple diagram to represent the architecture:

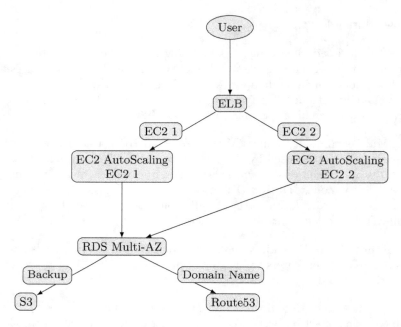

This architecture adheres to principles of a resilient system by providing:

- Redundancy: Through the use of ELB and Multi-AZ DB instances, we achieve process redundancy.

- Diversity: There is a diversity of resources to handle and process traffic coming from multiple sources.

- Modularity: The various components are well segregated, ensuring a fault in one does not affect the others. This also simplifies scaling individual components as needed.

- Adaptability: With AutoScaling in place, based on demand, the number of EC2 instances can be automatically increased or decreased.

- Prudence: Regular backups to S3 ensure that unforeseen data losses can be handled without major downtime.

In practice, the design and implementation of patterns for resilience in AWS or any cloud architecture can be more complex with considerations for security, cost optimization, and operational excellence. But this example gives a basic overview of how various AWS services can be combined to build a resilient system.

How can you test the resilience of an AWS application?

Building resilience into your applications on AWS is an integral part of robust and resilient architecture design. Testing the resilience of an AWS application involves proactively introducing failure into the system to verify that it continues to operate as intended during unexpected events. AWS provides different services and tools for testing, such as AWS Fault Injection Simulator, AWS Well-Architected Tool, AWS CloudWatch, etc. Here's some primary ways to test resilience:

Using AWS Fault Injection Simulator (FIS):

AWS FIS is a fully managed service that enables you to carry out fault injection experiments on your AWS environments. This service can help to test how prepared the applications are for random high-severity, low-frequency events.

It can inject different types of faults (like, API throttling, server failure, network latency, etc.) and check how your system reacts. By observing the process, you can make necessary modifications to your system to make it more resilient.

Automated testing:

Automated testing can validate whether the system is working as expected under both normal and failed conditions. AWS provides services like AWS CodePipeline and AWS CodeBuild to create, test, and deploy your applications.

Using the principles of Chaos Engineering:

Chaos Engineering is a principle where engineers intentionally introduce failures into the system to ensure that the system can still function under unpredictable conditions. Netflix's Chaos Monkey is a well-known tool for resilience testing in AWS cloud.

Monitoring and alerting:

You can use AWS CloudWatch for monitoring your application and setting alerts based on the application's behavior. AWS CloudTrail can record AWS API calls, and you can create alarms for particular events.

Important Metrics to track include:

- Error rates: The number of failed requests divided by the total requests during a given time period.

- Availability: The ability of a system to perform its required function over a stated period of time. Calculated using the formula: (Successful Requests) / (Successful Requests + Failed Requests)

- Latency: Time taken by a system to react to a given input or request.

- Throughput: Number of processes completed or details passed within the system in a given amount of time.

By using these testing methods and monitoring these underlying metrics, you can effectively measure how your system is likely to react under stress or if any part of the system fails, and make the necessary adjustments to improve the system's resilience. Remember, building resilience in your AWS applications is not a one-time activity but rather a continuous improvement and testing process.

3.4 Best Practices and Use Cases

What are some best practices for designing scalable and reliable systems on AWS?

Designing scalable and reliable systems on AWS does not happen by chance. It requires following best practices that will reduce downtime, increase efficiency, and provide a great user experience. Here are few best practices for designing scalable and reliable systems on AWS.

1. **Design for Failure**: Cloud architectures must be designed to be resilient even if some parts of the system fail. This can be achieved by implementing redundancy and replication, decoupling components to contain failures and limiting blast radius, and automating recovery processes.

Example: Use Multi-AZ (Availability Zones) deployment for Amazon RDS to ensure your database can failover to a standby replica in a different Availability Zone if the primary database fails.

2. **Implement Elasticity**: Use auto scaling and demand management to automatically scale resources up or down based on demand. Monitor system metrics and adjust capacity accordingly.

Example: Amazon EC2 Auto Scaling enables you to follow the demand curve for your applications, reducing the need for manual intervention.

3. **Leverage Different Storage Options**: AWS provides various storage options like Amazon S3 (object storage), Amazon EBS (block storage), and Amazon RDS (relational database service). Use the right type of storage for the specific use case.

Example: You could use Amazon S3 for storing and retrieving any amount of data at any time, from anywhere on the web.

4. **Loosely Couple Your Components**: Decouple your applica-

tions into smaller, loosely coupled components to ensure that they are failure isolated and can scale independently.

Example: Use Amazon SQS (Simple Queue Service) to decouple and scale microservices, distributed systems, and serverless applications.

5. **Security at All Levels**: Use the shared responsibility model. While AWS manages security of the cloud, customers are responsible for security in the cloud. Use Identity Access Management and VPC Security Groups, enable MFA (Multi-Factor Authentication), encrypt data at rest and in transit, and monitor activity with AWS CloudTrail.

Example: Use Amazon RDS encryption to secure your DB instances and snapshot data.

6. **Think Parallel**: Design the system to run operations in parallel to leverage the scalable nature of the cloud.

Example: Amazon EMR (Elastic MapReduce) can be used to process vast amounts of data in parallel.

7. **Continually Optimize Over Time**: Take advantage of the flexibility and large number of AWS services to continually refine and evolve your system. Perform regular audit of your resources and configurations and tune for improved performance, resilience and cost efficiency.

Example: Use AWS Cost Explorer to visualize, understand, and manage your AWS costs and usage over time.

Can you provide a real-life example where you implemented these best practices?

Suppose we were working on a project for a multinational company that needs to process massive amounts of data daily and wants to adopt cloud services for their machine learning endeavours. In this scenario, some specific best practices from Section 9.4 might be employed as follows:

1. **Design for scalability**

To accommodate the anticipated growth in the volume of data, the design of the architecture would allocate Elastic Map Reduce (EMR) clusters that auto-scales according to the data volume.

The auto-scaling rule might be something like:

Add 1 node when: CPU_Utilization > 70% in last 5 minutes

Remove 1 node when: CPU_Utilization < 20 % in last 20 minutes

2. **Leverage different storage options**

In this scenario, for data storage, Amazon S3 (Simple Storage Service) would be used providing cost-effective, scalable, and flexible object-storage.

For data analytics, Amazon Redshift, a highly scalable data warehousing service would be used. And for real-time processing use Amazon Kinesis, which can collect, process, and analyze video and data streams in real time.

3. **Design for Security**

AWS Identity and Access Management (IAM) could be used to control user access to AWS services and resources. The company's virtual private cloud (VPC) could be set up with private and public subnets, using security groups and network access control lists (NACLs) to restrict access at the instance and subnet level.

4. **Implement Serverless Architectures**

To further boost the efficiency and elasticity, use AWS Lambda (a serverless computing service) to run code for applications or backend services based on event triggers. For instance, a file upload to S3 bucket could trigger an AWS Lambda function to process the data.

5. **DevOps Practices**

Utilize AWS CodeCommit, CodeDeploy, CodePipeline, and Code-Build for source control, deployment, continuous integration and continuous delivery respectively. These services together can ensure seamless, automated, and efficient DevOps practices.

These practices combined would lead to the efficient and secure operation of the multinational company's big data processing and analytics efforts on AWS Cloud. The analytics and processing speed derived from this set up could help the company identify business trends and opportunities, thereby providing them significant competitive advantage in the marketplace.

What are some common use cases for scalable and reliable applications on AWS?

Amazon Web Services (AWS) offers a plethora of features and services that can be used to build scalable and reliable applications. Here are some common use cases:

1. Big Data Processing: AWS offers several big data tools such as Amazon EMR, Amazon Redshift, and AWS Glue. These services allow you to process, analyze, and visualize big data workloads in a scalable and reliable manner.

2. Content Delivery and Media Streaming: If you're building an application that requires streaming content such as video or music, AWS provides services like Amazon CloudFront and AWS Elemental Media Services.

3. Backup and Recovery: AWS offers services for data backup and disaster recovery, including Amazon S3, Amazon Glacier (now part of S3), and AWS Backup that give you the scalability and reliability you need for backup and recovery operations.

4. Machine Learning and AI: Services like Amazon SageMaker, AWS

Lambda, and AWS Lex can be used to build scalable machine learning and AI systems on the cloud.

5. Web Application Hosting: Amazon EC2, Amazon RDS, Amazon S3, and Amazon Elastic Beanstalk can be used to host scalable and reliable web applications.

6. Game Development and Hosting: With AWS Lambdas' serverless computing and Amazon GameLift's dedicated game server hosting, developers can focus on game creation without needing to manage infrastructure.

7. Internet of Things (IoT): AWS's IoT services (AWS IoT Core, AWS IoT Analytics etc.) provide advanced data analysis for devices, allowing for a smooth, scalable IoT experience.

Here's an example of how AWS can be used to create scalable architecture for web application hosting. Assume we are building a web application that consists of a front-end, a back-end, and a database.

- Front-end: For the front-end, we can use Amazon S3 to host the static web content and Amazon CloudFront for content delivery.

```
Amazon S3 (Scalable storage) --> Amazon CloudFront (Content Delivery Network)
```

- Back-end: The back-end logic can be hosted on EC2 instances that are managed by AWS Elastic Beanstalk.

```
User -> Amazon CloudFront -> AWS Elastic Beanstalk -> EC2 Instances
```

- Database: The database can be hosted on Amazon RDS, which will provide the necessary scalability and failover capabilities.

```
EC2 Instances -> Amazon RDS (Database service)
```

- To ensure reliability and fault-tolerance, these services can be spread across multiple availability zones.

The scalability of the system is achieved by using Elastic load balancers which distribute the network traffic accross multiple EC2 Instances, and with Auto Scaling groups, which manage the number of EC2 Instances, automatically adding and removing them according to demand.

```
Elastic Load Balancer -> Auto Scaling -> EC2 Instances
```

In conclusion, AWS provides a flexible and wide array of services to build scalable and reliable applications. From web application hosting and big data processing to machine learning and AI, the possibilities are practically endless.

How can you use AWS services together to create a scalable and reliable application?

To ensure that our application is scalable and reliable, we need to use several AWS services together. These services range from compute, to storage, to networking, to database, to management and governance, to security. Here are some AWS cloud service tools you can integrate and how they contribute to scalability and reliability:

1. **Amazon EC2 (Elastic Compute Cloud)**: EC2 is the backbone of AWS services, provides resizable virtual servers for hosting applications. Applications can automatically scale their capacity up and down depending on their needs using Auto Scaling Groups.

2. **Amazon RDS (Relational Database Service)**: Provides resizable and managed relational databases that easily scale capacity and throughput while also offering automated backups, software patching, and multiple availability zones for durability and high availability.

3. **Amazon S3 (Simple Storage Service)**: Provides scalable storage for any amount of data at any time. It also provides high durability, cross-region replication, and versioning for reliability.

4. **Amazon CloudFront**: A content delivery network (CDN) that caches content closer to users' locations, thereby increasing the speed of delivery and providing a seamless experience irrespective of user traffic.

5. **AWS Lambda**: This is a serverless compute service that lets you run your code without provisioning or managing servers. It can be triggered by other AWS services such as S3, RDS, or DynamoDB. This allows you to run your application in a scalable and reliable way without having to worry about the servers on which your application is running.

6. **Amazon DynamoDB**: A fast, reliable, and serverless NoSQL database service; it offers seamless scalability, serving any level of request traffic with single-digit millisecond latency.

7. **AWS Elastic Load Balancing (ELB)**: ELB automatically distributes incoming application traffic across multiple targets, such as Amazon EC2 instances, containers, IP addresses, and Lambda functions. It enhances reliability by ensuring that only healthy instances handle the traffic.

8. **Amazon Route 53**: A scalable and highly available Domain Name System (DNS). It routes end user requests to healthy endpoints of your application.

9. **AWS CloudWatch**: Monitors your resources and applications, collects and tracks metrics, and produces actionable insights. This aids consistent performance and operational health, contributing to reliability.

Here is an example of how these services are employed to create a scalable and reliable application:

- Web servers are hosted on Amazon EC2 instances, stored within an Auto Scaling group for scalability.

- Static contents (like Javascript, CSS, Images) are stored in Amazon S3 and delivered through Amazon CloudFront.

- Dynamic contents are stored in Amazon RDS or Amazon DynamoDB.

- Amazon Route 53 routes incoming traffic to either Amazon CloudFront (for static contents) or AWS ELB (for dynamic contents).

- AWS CloudWatch monitors the entire application.

By utilizing these services in conjunction with one another, applications can achieve high levels of scalability and reliability.

Note that the architecture and selection of AWS services will differ based on the specifics of your workload. You may also want to incorporate other services like AWS Step Functions for serverless workflows, AWS X-Ray for debugging and tracing, other managed services that make sense for your workload to further improve scalability and reliability.

What are some pitfalls to avoid when designing for scalability and reliability on AWS?

Designing for scalability and reliability on AWS involves multiple principles and strategies such as distributed systems, decoupled components, automatic scaling, caching, duplication, and fault-tolerant design.

Despite that, a few common pitfalls are often encountered:

1. **Not Designing for Failure:** AWS is designed to provide highly reliable and scalable services. However, failures can happen at any time. One common pitfall is not to consider potential failures and their impact on the system. To avoid this pitfall, implement strategies such as redundancy, replication, sharding, and maintaining a consistent state across all components in your failover strategy.

2. **Improper Capacity Planning:** Even though AWS offers autoscaling, some services still require you to provision capacity upfront. Failure to correctly estimate the capacity needs can lead to underutilized resources resulting in unnecessary cost or over-utilized resources

leading to poor performance and potential service disruption.

3. **Not Using Decoupled Architectures:** Tight coupling between components is another common pitfall. In a decoupled architecture, failure of a single component does not affect the other components. It's achieved using services like Amazon SQS or Kinesis. This also simplifies scaling as each component can scale independently.

4. **Neglecting Cost Optimization:** AWS services cost money, and without careful planning, costs can escalate quickly. To avoid this pitfall, use AWS cost management tools to track your spending and pay attention to cost optimization services like AWS Trusted Advisor.

5. **Ignoring Security Threats:** Security should be the foundation of any architecture. Despite AWS's built-in security, misconfigurations can lead to security vulnerabilities.

6. **Not Benchmarking Performance:** Without a performance baseline, identifying performance-related issues becomes a daunting task. Benchmark your application performance so you can identify any abnormal behavior.

7. **Improper Data Management:** Data retrieval should be minimized by distributed caching (Amazon ElastiCache). It saves cost and improves latency.

These principles are abstracted from the AWS well-architected framework that provides a consistent approach for customers and partners to evaluate architectures, and implement designs that can scale over time.

Can you discuss an example of a system that failed to scale or maintain reliability on AWS, and how the issue was addressed?

Let's discuss an example of a service that was built to handle a large number of incoming requests but ended up not being able to scale properly due to a few design decisions. This case will involve AWS DynamoDB, a fully-managed NoSQL database service.

Let's imagine a use case where an e-commerce company built a service for managing customer orders on top of DynamoDB. The customer orders were stored in a single DynamoDB table. This table used the customer ID as partition keys and the order creation timestamps as sort keys. As the business grew, the volume of customer orders increased substantially. However, the system started to suffer from high latency and occasional downtimes, which negatively affected the business.

Here is what went wrong:

Their AWS DynamoDB table had a emhot partitionem problem. DynamoDB partitions are storage units used by DynamoDB to divide the data and traffic for a table over sufficient server resources to meet throughput demands. Partitions are automatically managed by DynamoDB. But, DynamoDB scales based on the number of read/write capacity units that are evenly divided across the partitions. When you have a single or few customers with more orders than others (unbalanced write distribution), some partitions were getting hammered while others lay dormant (sporadic).

Now, here is how they addressed it to achieve scalability and reliability:

The solution was to use emDistributed Load Collectorsem, a technique which comprises adding a random suffix to the partition key value. Distributed Load Collector aims not only to distribute writes across multiple partition keys but also to enable high-speed reads by knowing the specific partition keys to retrieve the range of order data. Therefore, the hot partition problem was addressed efficiently.

But obviously, introducing random suffixes for partition key makes retrieving the total range of records for a single customer difficult. So they applied emDynamoDB Streamsem together with AWS Lambda. Whenever new data was written, the stream events triggered a Lambda function that arranged and aggregated order data in another DynamoDB table especially optimized for reads. It allowed quick lookups with the original semantics (CustomerID + DateTime).

Through these architectural changes, the solution achieved a just-right balance between write and read heavy operations, thus ensuring consistent performance and high availability of the service.

Please note that specific numeric details (e.g., the actual latency, the amount of data involved) would depend on the particular use case.

How can you ensure cost-effectiveness while designing for scalability and reliability on AWS?

Designing for scalability and reliability on AWS doesn't necessarily have to be expensive. There are a few best practices that you can use to ensure cost-effectiveness:

1. **Auto Scalability**: Auto Scaling provides an excellent way to optimize costs on AWS. In simple terms, it involves automatically scaling your resources based on demand. When there is more demand, your system automatically allocates more resources to handle the demand. When demand is low, these resources are scaled down to save costs. With Autoscaling, you simply pay for what you use, no more, no less.

2. **Right-Sizing**: Right-sizing means selecting the right instances types and sizes for your workload based on the specific requirements of your applications. Performing comprehensive assessments of your workloads and utilizing AWS' portfolio of instance types can help significantly reduce cost and improve efficiency.

3. **Spot Instances and Reserved Instances**: Spot Instances can be purchased at a much lower price than regular EC2 instances. They can be used for various use cases like data analysis, batch jobs, background processing, and optional tasks. Reserved Instances provide a capacity reservation, which offers significant cost savings compared to using on-demand instances.

4. **Storage Class Analysis and Lifecycle Configuration**: By analyzing your storage access patterns and setting up lifecycle configuration rules, you can transition your object storage to cheaper storage classes to save costs.

5. **Delete Unattached resources**: Often, resources that are detached from their main resources (e.g., EBS volumes that are not attached to EC2 instances) are left running, which continue to be billed. Deleting these can provide significant cost savings.

6. **Bulk purchasing**: AWS offers discounts for bulk purchasing. Larger, upfront purchases might seem more expensive in the short term, but it drastically reduces running costs in the long term.

7. **Caching**: Implementing effective caching strategies can reduce the load on your databases and thus decrease read and write costs.

8. **Cost Explorer and Budgets**: AWS also provides tools like Cost Explorer and budgets to track your costs and usage over time. Regularly reviewing this data can help identify cost-saving opportunities.

Remember, designing for cost-effectiveness oftentimes is not a one-time operation but should be an ongoing operational activity. Regular review and optimization of your resources is a must to ensure cost-effectiveness continuously.

Actual implementation may vary depending on the specifics of the workload and business requirements. However, these best practices provide a strong foundation for cost-effective design on AWS.

What are some considerations for designing a scalable and reliable application that needs to operate across multiple regions?

Designing a scalable and reliable application that needs to operate across multiple regions requires careful planning and execution. The strategy has to consider aspects like data replication, latency, services availability in each region, cost, and legislation.

Here are some important considerations:

1. **Data Replication:** An important aspect of making an application available across multiple regions is data replication. Amazon offers services like Amazon RDS (Relational Database Service) and DynamoDB Global Tables for data replication across regions. The method of replication (synchronous vs asynchronous) has to be selected based on the application requirements. Synchronous replication has lower latency but higher cost, whereas asynchronous replication is cheaper but may lead to data inconsistencies.

2. **Latency:** Applications running across multiple regions may face latency issues. This is because the distance between the user and the region where the application is being served can affect the response time. To solve this, AWS provides services like Route 53 (DNS service) and CloudFront (CDN service) to route users to the nearest region and cache application content at edge locations, reducing latency.

3. **Service Availability:** Not all AWS services are available in all regions. Thus, the selection of regions should be made based on the required services for the application. AWS provides a "Region Table" that shows the availability of services in different regions.

4. **Cost:** Different regions have different pricing for AWS services. Regions like 'us-east-1' are generally cheaper than others like 'ap-south-1'. Therefore, cost can be a key consideration in the selection of regions.

5. **Legislation and Data Sovereignty:** Sometimes, the location of data storage is regulated by law. For example, the GDPR requires personal data of EU citizens to be stored in the EU unless certain conditions are met. In this case, you might need to carefully choose your regions to comply with data sovereignty laws.

Here are examples of topologies for multi-regional applications:

- **Active-passive topology:** In this configuration, all traffic is served by the primary region. In the event of a failure, the application fails over to the secondary region. Suitable for applications that can tolerate some downtime, the mechanism can be automated using Route53 health checks.

- **Active-active topology:** In this configuration, the application traffic is distributed across all regions. This setup provides lower latency, higher availability, and better fault tolerance. However, it needs careful management of data replication and consistency. AWS services like DynamoDB Global Tables and S3 Cross-Region Replication can help to manage this.

In sum, designing a scalable and reliable multi-regional application involves trade-offs and careful selection of regions, data replication strategies, DNS and CDN configurations, and failsafe mechanisms. The AWS well-architected framework provides a comprehensive guide towards achieving this.

How would you approach the task of migrating an existing, less scalable or reliable system onto AWS?

Migrating an existing, less scalable or reliable system onto AWS involves a strategic framework known as the AWS Cloud Adoption Framework (CAF). This approach guides your organization through the transition to a cloud-based infrastructure. While we should really be performing the AIOps analysis for the exact details, here is a general overview:

1. **Gap Analysis:** This step involves understanding the current state of your system, evaluating the desired state in AWS, and identifying differences. Analyzing the gap determines how to successfully migrate or rebuild services, databases, applications, etc. onto AWS.

2. **Planning your migration approach:** Design your AWS architecture taking into account AWS proven best practices like Security, Reliability, Performance Efficiency, Operational Excellence and

Cost Optimization. Some solutions can be migrated with minimal changes (re-hosting or 'lift and shift'), others might need some level of modification in drive mode (re-platforming or 'lift, tinker, and shift) and some might need to be completely reimagined and rearchitected (refactoring or 're-architecting').

3. **Proof of concept (POC):** Build a POC on AWS for familiarization with the systems and services. This assists in overcoming the challenges that may arise while migrating the whole system.

4. **Data Migration:** Use AWS services like Database Migration Service (DMS), S3 Transfer Acceleration or AWS Snowball to move data. The method will depend on data size, network speed, security needs among other factors.

5. **Applications and Services Migration:** Deploy systems in a phased manner to minimize the risk of any business disruptions.

6. **Testing:** Regular tests to verify that the migrated system meets operational, security, performance, and business requirements.

7. **Optimize and Scale:** Once all components of the system are migrated, it's time to optimize your architecture for better scalability, security, reliability, cost efficiency and performance.

Specific use case can be an ecommerce business needing a sudden scalability due to increased online activity. Migrating to AWS cloud will allow them on-demand scalability with services like Auto Scaling and Elastic Load Balancer. In addition to that they could also leverage Aurora for DB that enables up to 15 read replicas to handle increasing customer data requests. This could enhance reliability and availability of their platform.

AWS CAF organizes guidance into six areas of focus, called perspectives: Business, People, Governance, Platform, Security, and Operations. These perspectives involve an integral part of the overall IT portfolio and require consideration when moving to the cloud. So, as a part of best practices, organizations need to keep these points in mind when migrating to the cloud.

Please note that AWS's Well-Architected Framework (WAF) is also a crucial reference guide during your migration. WAF helps cloud architects to build the most secure, high-performing, resilient, and efficient infrastructure possible for their applications.

This approach can be presented as flow in a form of flowchart:

Gap Analysis ↓
Migration Planning ↓
POC ↓
Data Migration ↓
App/Services Migration ↓
Testing ↓
Optimize & Scale

In conclusion, migrating an existing system onto AWS is not just about moving an application or database from point A to B. Rather, it's a transformational process that involves strategic planning, execution, and continuous optimization.

Can you discuss a case where a well-designed AWS application successfully handled a dramatic increase in load or recovered from a major failure?

Netflix is known for its high levels of daily traffic, reaching millions of subscribers across the globe. However, they experience even more substantial traffic spikes during the launch of highly anticipated series or when they're conducting large marketing campaigns. To manage these unpredictable and hefty traffic loads, Netflix turned to AWS's cloud services.

Netflix's architecture on AWS is designed to be self-healing and resilient. They have adopted a microservice architecture on AWS where each functionality — such as recommendations, customer profiles, etc. — is a separate service, allowing for better fault isolation. Each of these microservices is replicated across multiple AWS Availability Zones (AZs) for high availability.

In the event of a sudden traffic surge, Netflix uses AWS Auto Scaling groups to automatically adjust the number of EC2 (Elastic Compute Cloud) instances in response to conditions you specify. For example, you could stipulate that CPU utilization for your EC2 instances should stay around 60%. When the load goes beyond this point, new instances will be automatically launched, and when the load drops, it will terminate the unused instances.

Netflix also make use of AWS Elastic Load Balancing to distribute incoming application traffic across the multiple EC2 instances which optimizes the performance.

In addition to these techniques, Netflix developed a tool called "Chaos Monkey" that intentionally tries to cause failures in their production environment during business hours. The purpose of this is to constantly test their ability to survive common types of failure without any customer impact. These rigorous tests ensure that they're always prepared for real-world scenarios.

Here's a simplified diagram showing Netflix's AWS microservice architecture:

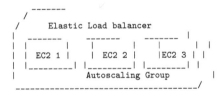

Note: In real deployment, each of these components would be replicated across multiple Availability Zones.

This kind of robust cloud architecture has not only empowered Netflix to smoothly handle the dramatic fluctuation in traffic loads, but also allowed them to automatically recover from failures rapidly. With such practices, Netflix was able to ensure uninterrupted service to its subscribers, even when facing unexpected glitches or demand spikes. Similarly, these AWS best practices can also be adopted by other companies who want to create a resilient and high-performing cloud architecture.

Chapter 4

Security Considerations for AWS

Security in the digital age, particularly on platforms like AWS, is paramount. Chapter 10 delves deep into the myriad security considerations one must address when deploying and maintaining systems on AWS. The journey commences with a detailed look at Identity and Access Management (IAM), AWS's comprehensive service that allows administrators to define and manage user access to resources. As the narrative unfolds, the focus shifts to network security within AWS, elucidating the strategies, tools, and best practices to safeguard infrastructure and data. Ensuring that readers are not just reactive but proactive, the chapter concludes with an overarching view of security best practices on AWS. These guidelines are geared towards enabling architects and developers to design and operate secure applications and infrastructures, ensuring that vulnerabilities are minimized and that systems remain robust against ever-evolving threats.

4.1 Identity and Access Management (IAM)

What is IAM and why is it important for security in AWS?

IAM, which stands for Identity and Access Management, is a feature provided by Amazon Web Services (AWS) for managing access to AWS resources and services. IAM enables you to manage users, security credentials such as access keys, and permissions that control which AWS resources users and applications can access.

IAM has the following key features which makes it important for security in AWS:

1.) Fine-Grained Access Control: IAM allows for fine-grained access control to AWS resources. For example, you can create an IAM policy that grants a user permission to use only a specific subset of transitions in an AWS service.

2.) AWS Multi-Factor Authentication (MFA): IAM supports multi-factor authentication (MFA) for privileged accounts, adding an additional layer of security over the simple username/password scheme.

3.) Integration with AWS services: IAM is integrated with various AWS services, meaning it's used as the primary mechanism for controlling access to these services.

4.) Identity Federation: IAM supports identity federation, which means you can grant outside identities permissions to AWS resources without having to create an IAM user.

5.) Policy Conditions: IAM policies can specify conditions for when actions are allowed or denied. For example, a policy could specify that an action is allowed only if it occurs from a specific IP range.

IAM is a crucial part of securing AWS resources, as it provides the necessary tools to ensure that only authorized users and applications are granted access to your AWS resources.

Let's consider an example: consider an organization with multiple departments such as HR, Sales, and Finance. Each of these departments engage with different AWS resources. IAM can be used to create users and user groups specific to these departments, and define access policies to AWS resources accordingly. For instance, the Finance user group might have access to AWS Billing, while the HR user group may have access to AWS WorkDocs.

IAM roles can also be used to delegate permissions or grant access to AWS resources to AWS services or applications running on EC2 instances, without having to share long-term credentials. This not only enhances security by adhering to the principle of least privilege, but also significantly reduces the operational burden of managing credentials for applications.

Therefore IAM, with its ability to manage access to AWS resources in a fine-grained, safe, and controlled manner, is crucial for maintaining the security of AWS environments.

Can you describe the concept of users, groups, and roles in IAM?

AWS Identity and Access Management (IAM) is a web service that helps you securely control access to AWS resources for your users. It includes several elements for managing access, key among them being Users, Groups, and Roles.

Users An IAM user is an identity with AWS credentials associated with it. This can represent a person, an application, or a service that uses those credentials for AWS interactions.

Each IAM user is unique within the AWS account and is associated with individual security credentials that dictate their permissions. For example, a user could be given permissions to read data from an

S3 bucket but not write data. This is specified by the AWS policy associated with the user.

Groups In AWS IAM, you can create groups, which are collections of IAM users. Groups help simplify permission management as you can assign permissions to a group, and all users in that group will inherit those permissions.

For example, if you have a group of developers who need the same permissions, you can create a 'Developers' group, provide the necessary permissions to this group, and then add all the developers to this group. If a new developer joins the team, you simply add them to the 'Developers' group instead of manually attaching the necessary permissions.

Roles Roles in AWS IAM are similar to users, in that they are AWS identities with permission policies determining what the identity can and cannot do. However, IAM users have a long-term set of security credentials stored with the user, roles do not.

IAM roles are a secure way to grant permissions to entities that you trust. Examples of entities include the following:

- An IAM user in another AWS account

- An application code running on an EC2 instance that needs to perform actions on AWS resources

- An AWS service that needs to act on resources in your account to enhance your service experience

Essentially, instead of sharing your security credentials (the keys), you delegate access to AWS resources to these entities by giving them roles.

To summarize, IAM roles, users, and groups help manage your AWS security landscape by enabling fine-grained access control to your AWS resources.

What is a policy in AWS IAM and how is it used to control access?

In AWS Identity and Access Management (IAM), a policy is essentially a set of permissions that dictate what actions are allowed or denied on various AWS resources. It is a crucial component of the AWS security model and plays a significant role in managing access control for your AWS environment.

A policy is written in JSON (JavaScript Object Notation) format and it specifies the permissions in terms of '"Effect"', '"Action"', '"Resource"', and '"Condition"'. Here are their explanations:

1. '"Effect"': The Effect can either be '"Allow"' or '"Deny"'. '"Allow"' means the actions specified in the '"Action"' element are allowed for the resources in the '"Resource"' element. '"Deny"' means the opposite.

2. '"Action"': The Action element is where you specify the specific AWS service operations (like s3:CreateBucket, sqs:SendMessage) that you want to allow or deny.

3. '"Resource"': In the Resource element, you specify the resources that the statement applies to.

4. '"Condition"': The Condition element (which is optional) is where you can specify conditions for when the policy statement is in effect.

Here is an example of a policy:

```
{
  "Version": "2012-10-17",
  "Statement": [
    {
      "Effect": "Allow",
      "Action": "s3:ListBucket",
      "Resource": "arn:aws:s3:::example_bucket"
    },
    {
      "Effect": "Allow",
      "Action": ["s3:PutObject", "s3:GetObject", "s3:DeleteObject"],
      "Resource": "arn:aws:s3:::example_bucket/*"
    },
```

```
  {
    "Effect": "Deny",
    "Action": "s3:*",
    "Resource": "*",
    "Condition": {"Bool": {"aws:secureTransport": false}}
  }
 ]
}
```

In this example policy, there are three statements that:

1. Allow the user to list the items in 'example_bucket'.

2. Allow the user to perform put, get, and delete operations on objects within 'example_bucket'.

3. Deny all other S3 actions when the request is not made using SSL.

Policies in AWS cannot grant more permissions than those that are permitted by other permissions policies. This implies that one can restrict permissions but not extend them through a policy. For instance, if a user has permissions to perform all actions in the IAM service but a policy only allows reading from a particular service, the net permission of the user will be: they only have read access to the said service.

Policies can be associated either with a user or a group or a role, hence providing flexibility for managing access control. For example, one could create a policy that grants read access to an S3 bucket and then attach it with a user or a group of users or a role. The user (or users or role) will then inherit the permissions defined in the policy.

How would you secure access keys in AWS?

Securing access keys in AWS involves several steps including regular key rotation, ensuring proper access levels, and secure storage. Here's the comprehensive step-by-step guide to securing access keys in AWS.

Regular Rotation: Regularly rotating AWS access keys can help limit the impact if keys are compromised. AWS recommends that you rotate the keys every 90 days at minimum but the best practice is to rotate keys every 30-45 days. Here is a Python script that makes use of Boto3, the AWS SDK for Python, to delete an access key and then create a new one for a user:

```python
import boto3

def rotate_access_keys(user_name):
    client = boto3.client('iam')
    response = client.list_access_keys(UserName=user_name)

    for key_metadata in response['AccessKeyMetadata']:
        response = client.delete_access_key(UserName=user_name,
            AccessKeyId=key_metadata['AccessKeyId'])

    client.create_access_key(UserName=user_name)

rotate_access_keys('YourUserName')
```

Least Privilege Principle: Users should have the minimal access necessary to perform their job roles. This can greatly reduces the attack surface if a set of credentials is ever compromised. AWS Identity and Access Management (IAM) allows fine-tuned access control to your AWS resources. Instead of giving a user full permissions, you create policies with permissions and then attach them to the IAM user. An example on how to do this is as follows:

```json
{
  "Version": "2012-10-17",
  "Statement": [
    {
      "Effect": "Allow",
      "Action": "s3:PutObject",
      "Resource": "arn:aws:s3:::mybucket/*"
    }
  ]
}
```

This policy only allows a user to upload objects to a specified S3 bucket.

Key Storage: Access keys should be stored securely and should never be embedded in code or checked into a version control system. Ideally, access keys should be stored in an encrypted format in a secure server or using a secret management system such as AWS Secrets Manager or AWS Systems Manager Parameter Store.

Monitor Usage: Use AWS CloudTrail to log, continuously monitor and retain events related to API calls across your AWS infrastructure. This can help identify unusual activity such as access attempts at unusual times, large numbers of requests, or requests from unusual locations.

MFA: Use Multi-Factor Authentication (MFA) for users that will use access keys. This adds an extra layer of protection for access key usage.

Password Policy: Implement a strong password policy. IAM lets you configure a password policy for your AWS account, you can specify password complexity requirements and mandatory rotation periods.

Remember to keep in mind that not all AWS services support using access keys. In cases like these, you should manage AWS service access through IAM roles.

How does multi-factor authentication (MFA) work in AWS?

Multi-Factor Authentication (MFA) on AWS provides an extra level of security that you can apply to your AWS environment. It requires users to present two separate forms of identification:

1. Something you know (a password or passphrase).
2. Something you have (a trusted device that's not easily duplicated).

The second form of identification is a number that's automatically generated by a device that you can secure in a physical location.

With MFA, even if a password (the first factor) is compromised, an attacker still won't be able to access the system without being able to generate the correct second factor, which makes breaching your AWS resources much more difficult.

Amazon supports several types of MFA devices, including:

- Virtual MFA devices.

- Hardware MFA devices.

- SMS text message-based MFA devices.

- U2F security keys.

The basic process to authenticate using multi-factor authentication (MFA) is as follows:

1. You first sign in to an AWS website by using your AWS account root user name and password. 2. On the next page, you are prompted to enter a six-digit single-use code from your MFA device.

Let's consider the Virtual MFA devices. These devices run a software application that generates six-digit authentication codes. They include smartphone applications, key fobs and display cards.

Here is the sequence of steps while using a virtual MFA device:

The authenticating device generates an 8-byte (64-bit) HMAC-SHA1 cryptographic hash function.

This value, along with the timestamp, is used to generate a six-digit one-time password (OTP).

The OTP is sent to the MFA device.

The user enters the OTP into the authentication response.

The authenticating device confirms the OTP, and if it matches, allows the user access.

The authentication server and the MFA device both create HMAC-SHA1 values, which must match. The critical point is that this process uses a shared secret key for the username in question. The timing for code generation is done at 30-second intervals.

In terms of AWS IAM, you can use MFA in several ways:

- For your root account: It is highly recommended to enable MFA for your AWS account's root user.

- For individual IAM users: You can enable MFA for each IAM user in your account.

- For access to AWS services and resources through MFA-protected API access.

To implement MFA, you will need to adjust your IAM policy to require MFA, and your users will need to configure MFA devices using the IAM console.

The IAM policy that enforces MFA might look like this:

```
{
  "Version": "2012-10-17",
  "Statement": [
    {
      "Sid": "AllowAllUsersToListAccounts",
      "Effect": "Allow",
      "Action": "iam:ListUsers",
      "Resource": "*"
    },
    {
      "Sid": "AllowIndividualUserToListOnlyTheirOwnAccount",
      "Effect": "Allow",
      "Action": "iam:ListAccountAliases",
      "Resource": "*",
      "Condition": {
        "Bool": { "aws:MultiFactorAuthPresent": true }
      }
    }
  ]
}
```

This policy allows all users to perform 'iam:ListUsers'. However, the second statement allows users to perform 'iam:ListAccountAliases' only if they have authenticated with MFA.

Remember, handling AWS MFA requires careful security consideration and proper enforcement of IAM Policies, IAM Roles and AWS Security Best Practices.

Can you explain the principle of least privilege and how it applies to IAM?

The principle of least privilege (PoLP) is a computer security concept in which a user is given the minimum levels of access – or permissions – necessary to complete his/her job functions. Essentially, the principle implies that a system is better off when its modules (like processes, users, and programs) are given just enough privileges to perform their work, but no more.

This principle can mitigate potential damage if a module ever becomes compromised, as the scope of actions the module could perform would be limited to its necessary functions and nothing more.

When applied to AWS Identity and Access Management (IAM), the PoLP increases the overall security of your AWS resources. You can achieve this by only granting the permissions necessary to perform a task. For example, you can create different IAM users for diverse individual tasks rather than giving administrative permissions to a single, general IAM user. If an IAM user requires additional AWS access to fulfill their task, you can grant that permission as needed.

Policy Evaluation Logic

IAM determines whether a request is allowed or denied by using policy evaluation logic. Here's a step-by-step guide:

1. If there's an explicit deny, IAM returns a "Deny" decision. No other policies are evaluated.

2. If there's at least one explicit allow, IAM returns an "Allow" decision. Otherwise, it goes to the next step.

3. If there are no explicit allow or deny statements, IAM returns a "Deny" decision.

To ensure all IAM users follow the PoLP, you should analyze your AWS environment and understand each user's job requirements. Thereafter, you can delegate precise permissions to each IAM user, thus minimizing potential exploits.

This principle, by constraining the capabilities of the users to minimal privileges necessary, reduces the chances of an unwanted entity getting access to critical operations or sensitive data within AWS.

How can IAM roles help in maintaining security when using AWS services from within an EC2 instance?

IAM roles provide a secure way to grant permissions to EC2 instances to make service requests on behalf of the instance's associated services without the need to share or manage security credentials like access keys.

To better understand how this plays out in a practical AWS setting, let's consider an example. Suppose you have an EC2 instance that needs to read objects from an S3 bucket. Instead of embedding AWS Access Keys within the EC2 instance (which could potentially be exposed or leaked), you can instead assign an IAM role to the EC2 instance at the time of creation. The IAM role has policies defining what permissions the EC2 instances should have, which in this case would be read access to the specified S3 bucket.

Here is how it works:

1. An IAM role is created in AWS IAM with the desired set of permissions (access to S3 bucket in this case).

2. The IAM role is then associated with the EC2 instance during its creation.

3. AWS then automatically provides temporary credentials to the EC2 instance that are cyclically rotated. These credentials are used

by services or applications on the instance to make authorized AWS service requests.

Effectively, IAM roles eliminate the need to share or store sensitive AWS access keys and secret access keys.

Furthermore, based on the principle of least privilege (POLP), with IAM roles, you can grant fine-grained access, i.e., only required permissions, to your applications, thus preventing unnecessary exposure to other services.

Use of IAM roles also enhances auditability. IAM roles leave access trails for services they interact with in AWS CloudTrail, thus, if something goes wrong, these trails can be followed back to the responsible source.

Finally, IAM roles can be switched during runtime without having to stop or start EC2 instances, offering flexibility and convenience when situations require changing permissions.

For instance, here's how you would attach an IAM role to an EC2 instance using AWS CLI:

```
aws ec2 associate-iam-instance-profile --region us-west-1
        --instance-id i-0abcdef1234567890 --iam-instance-profile Name="MyIAMRole"
```

In summary, using IAM roles with EC2 instances promotes better security practices by eliminating the need to manage AWS keys, enabling fine-grained access control, improving auditability, and providing the flexibility to change roles without disruption.

Can you provide an example of setting up a complex IAM policy?

Let's discuss an example of a complex IAM policy in AWS. IAM (Identity and Access Management) policies are a way of managing access rights for your AWS resources. It's important to note that there are multiple ways to write IAM policies; however, the recommended approach is to follow the principle of least privilege (POLP). POLP means giving a user or a role only those access rights that are necessary to carry out their job function, nothing more, nothing less.

Let's take an example here. Suppose we have an AWS S3 bucket resource and we need to build an IAM policy that allows:

1. UserGroupA to have complete access.

2. UserGroupB to upload objects to the bucket only.

3. UserGroupC to list and download objects from the bucket.

4. UserGroupD to modify only the bucket policy.

With these requirements, the policy may look something like:

```
{
    "Version": "2012-10-17",
    "Statement": [
        {
            "Sid": "FullAccess",
            "Effect": "Allow",
            "Principal": {
                "AWS": "arn:aws:iam::ACCOUNT-ID-WITHOUT-HYPHENS:usergroup/
                    UserGroupA"
            },
            "Action": "s3:*",
            "Resource": [
                "arn:aws:s3:::bucket-name",
                "arn:aws:s3:::bucket-name/*"
            ]
        },
        {
            "Sid": "UploadOnly",
            "Effect": "Allow",
            "Principal": {
                "AWS": "arn:aws:iam::ACCOUNT-ID-WITHOUT-HYPHENS:usergroup/
                    UserGroupB"
            },
            "Action": "s3:PutObject",
            "Resource": "arn:aws:s3:::bucket-name/*"
        },
        {
            "Sid": "ListandGetObject",
            "Effect": "Allow",
            "Principal": {
                "AWS": "arn:aws:iam::ACCOUNT-ID-WITHOUT-HYPHENS:usergroup/
                    UserGroupC"
            },
            "Action": [
                "s3:GetObject",
                "s3:ListBucket"
```

```
            ],
            "Resource": [
                "arn:aws:s3:::bucket-name",
                "arn:aws:s3:::bucket-name/*"
            ]
        },
        {
            "Sid": "ChangePolicy",
            "Effect": "Allow",
            "Principal": {
                "AWS": "arn:aws:iam::ACCOUNT-ID-WITHOUT-HYPHENS:usergroup/
                    UserGroupD"
            },
            "Action": "s3:PutBucketPolicy",
            "Resource": "arn:aws:s3:::bucket-name"
        }
    ]
}
```

This IAM policy contains five main elements:

1. Sid (Statement ID): An optional identifier that you provide for the policy statement.

2. Effect: Whether the statement will "Allow" or "Deny" access.

3. Principal: The user that is allowed or denied access to a resource (could also be a role or account).

4. Action: The operations that the user is allowed or denied access to.

5. Resource: The AWS resource that the action applies to.

Please replace "ACCOUNT-ID-WITHOUT-HYPHENS", "bucket-name", and "usergroup" with your actual AWS account ID, S3 bucket name, and the user group's ARN.

This policy allows UserGroupA full access to the S3 bucket, allows UserGroupB to only upload (PutObject) to the bucket, allows User-GroupC to list the bucket and download (GetObject) objects from it, and allows UserGroupD to modify (PutBucketPolicy) the bucket policy only.

What are IAM roles for service accounts (IRSA) and where are they used?

IAM roles for service accounts (IRSA) is a feature in AWS that lets you assign an IAM role directly to a Kubernetes service account. It refers to a mechanism in AWS Identity and Access Management (IAM) that allows an administrator to delegate permissions to an AWS service or entity to make service requests on behalf of the user.

Under normal circumstances, applications deployed in a Kubernetes cluster would need to use the IAM credentials attached to underlying nodes or the ones hardcoded in the application to interact with other AWS services. This approach has a few drawbacks including security risks with extensive permissions and the operational overhead of credentials management.

The IRSA feature addresses this by creating a role that is tied to a specific Kubernetes service account. This way, the service account can possess only the permissions required by associated pods, dramatically reducing the risk of excessive permissions. When an application tries to interact with an AWS service, the AWS SDK in the application fetches temporary credentials for the role tied to the service account. It means that applications don't need to handle credentials management and also there are no long-term credentials which boosts security.

For example, let's say you have a Kubernetes-based application that needs to interact with an Amazon S3 bucket. Instead of attaching the required IAM roles to the nodes or hardcoding AWS credentials in the application, you can use IRSA to assign an IAM role directly to your Kubernetes service account. Any pods run from that service account will thus have the required permissions to access the S3 bucket.

Here's how you may provide IAM roles for service accounts:

1. Create an IAM OIDC identity provider for your cluster

2. Create an IAM role and establish a trust relationship with the service account

3. Associate the IAM role with the service account

4. Deploy the pod with the Kubernetes service account

As per the application of IRSA, it is used in the Amazon Elastic Kubernetes Service (EKS) to ensure that applications running on the platform have the appropriate level of access to AWS resources.

The major benefits of IRSA include:

- It allows for the least privilege principle, providing only necessary access to perform the required tasks.

- It removes the need to provide access to the underlying hosts' role.

- Using Kubernetes service accounts to manage IAM credentials simplifies credential management.

- With IRSA, credentials are temporary and rotated automatically, thereby improving security.

- It enhances auditing by allowing individual application-level audit trails.

In conclusion, IAM Roles for Service Accounts is a secure and efficient way of managing AWS permissions for applications running on EKS or any Kubernetes service on AWS.

How can you audit the use of IAM credentials?

AWS offers several services that can be leveraged to audit the use of Identity and Access Management (IAM) credentials. Specifically, you would typically use AWS CloudTrail, AWS Config, and/or AWS IAM Access Analyzer.

AWS CloudTrail

This is a service that provides event history of your AWS account activity, including actions taken through the AWS Management Console, AWS SDKs, command line tools, and other AWS services. This event history simplifies security analysis, resource change tracking, and troubleshooting.

Here's how AWS CloudTrail works for auditing IAM:

- AWS CloudTrail logs API activity in AWS accounts. It captures API calls made on your account and delivers the log files to an Amazon S3 bucket that you've specified. This includes calls from the AWS Management Console and from code calls to the API operations.

- Any AWS action (such as using the console, CLI, or AWS SDKs to provision, modify or terminate resources) is an API operation. When an IAM user in your account places an API call, CloudTrail captures who made the request, when was it made, what was requested, and the outcome of the call, among other things.

- You can then use these logs to analyze and visualize API call activity with tools such as AWS CloudWatch, Amazon Athena and Amazon QuickSight, or with your own analytics solutions.

AWS Config

AWS Config provides resource inventory, configuration history, and configuration change notifications to enable security and governance. You can use AWS Config Rules enables you to create rules that automatically check the configuration of AWS resources recorded by AWS Config.

For IAM auditing, you can use AWS Config to:

- Keep track of the configuration history of your IAM resources.

- Determine your overall compliance against the rules according to AWS Config.

- Review changes in configurations and relationships between IAM resources.

- Determine detailed resource configuration attributes.

IAM Access Analyzer

AWS IAM Access Analyzer helps you identify the resources in your organization and accounts, such as Amazon S3 buckets or IAM roles, that are shared with an external entity. It provides details about the accessing entity or the accessed resource.

For IAM auditing, you can get an overview of who has access to which resource. For example, it could notify you if the permissions of a certain IAM role were changed to grant access to an unexpected external entity.

With these tools you can gain visibility into when, why, and where IAM credentials were used, and whether their usage complies with your organization's best practices. This helps enable effective governance and risk auditing of your AWS resources.

IAM audit process generally followed these steps:

- Keep track of IAM access keys (with AWS CloudTrail).

- Enable MFA (multi-factor authentication) for privileged users.

- Regularly rotate (change) IAM credentials.

- Remove unnecessary credentials.

- Use policy conditions for improved security.

- Monitor activity in your AWS account.

Also, some more advanced techniques like enforcing least privilege, and secure credential storage are recommended.

4.2   Network Security in AWS

How does AWS VPC contribute to network security?

Amazon Virtual Private Cloud (VPC) is an essential component for network security in AWS. VPC provides a secure, custom-defined virtual network within the AWS cloud, giving users control over their virtual networking environment including selection of IP address range, creation of subnets, and configuration of route tables and network gateways.

Here are some key ways in which AWS VPC contributes to network security:

1. **Security Groups and Network Access Control Lists (ACLs)**: Security groups work at the instance level. They control inbound and outbound traffic at the operating system level. In contrast, Network ACLs operate at the subnet level, controlling access to ranges of IP addresses within the VPC.

2. **Subnet and Route tables**: When dividing your VPC IP address range into multiple segments (subnets), you can design public-facing (internet-facing) and private-facing subnets. Route tables enable traffic flow between subnets and to gateways. By isolating different environments into different subnets, you can reduce the exposure of more sensitive parts of your architecture.

3. **Internet Gateways and NAT Gateways**: Internet Gateways (IGWs) allow communication between your VPC and the internet. Network Address Translation (NAT) Gateways allow outbound-only internet from instances that are inside private subnets. NAT gateways prevent the internet from initiating a connection with the instances.

4. **VPN and Direct Connect**: AWS provides virtual private network (VPN) and AWS Direct Connect options to securely connect your existing networks to VPCs.

5. **VPC Peering**: VPC Peering allows secure and private connection between different VPCs, even across different regions. This enhances security as traffic does not traverse public internet.

6. **Flow Logs**: Flow logs capture information about the IP traffic going to and from network interfaces in your VPC to monitor and troubleshoot how your network is accessed and used.

7. **VPC Endpoints**: VPC endpoints enable private connectivity between your VPC and supported AWS services without requiring access over the Internet, through a NAT device, VPN connection, or AWS Direct Connect connection.

Here's a simple illustration of how these aspects work together.

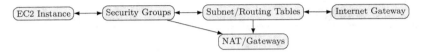

In conclusion, all these utilities work in conjunction to build a layer of security, ensuring that unauthorized access is denied while authorized communication happens smoothly. Moreover, the user can customize security settings according to their specific requirements. AWS VPC, therefore, contributes crucially to an organization's network security in AWS. (source: AWS documentation)

What are security groups and network access control lists (ACLs) in AWS?

Security Groups and Network Access Control Lists (ACLs) are two types of firewall protection provided by AWS to secure the resources within a Virtual Private Cloud (VPC).

Security Groups:

Security Groups act as a virtual firewall for your Amazon EC2 instances to control incoming and outgoing traffic. They operate at the instance level. In other words, they apply on a per-instance basis. If a particular security group bound to an instance allows specific IP or Port, then that rule will apply to all instances associated with that security group.

The rules of the Security Groups are **stateful**, meaning any change in inbound rules will automatically reflect in the outbound rules. For example, if you allow an incoming request, the outgoing

	Security Groups	Network ACLs
Operate at	Instance Level	Subnet Level
State	Stateful	Stateless
Rule Evaluation	All rules evaluated together	Rules are numbered and evaluated in order starting with the lowest number.
Type of Rules	Allow only	Allow and Deny

reply is automatically allowed, regardless of outbound rules.

Rules include allow rules only, and these rules can protect both inbound and outbound traffic. There are no deny rules for security groups.

Network Access Control Lists (ACLs):

Network ACLs operate at the subnet level and provide an additional layer of security, acting as a virtual firewall for controlling traffic in and out of one or more subnets. Every VPC by default has a modifiable default ACL that allows all inbound and outbound traffic.

The rules of Network ACLs are **stateless**, meaning we have to explicitly allow the inbound and outbound traffic i.e., if we allow an incoming request, we would have to add a rule to allow the outgoing reply.

Network ACLs have separate inbound and outbound rules, and each rule can either allow or deny traffic.

Here is a comparison table:

Simply put, Security Groups are like your instance's personal firewall, while Network ACLs is the virtual border guard of your subnets. They work together to provide a two-tiered security mechanism for your AWS infrastructure.

Can you explain how a subnet works in AWS?

A subnet, or subnetwork, is a logical subdivision of an IP network. The practice of dividing a network into two or more networks is called subnetting. AWS provides two types of subnetting one is Public which allow the internet to access the machine and another is private which is hidden from the internet.

In AWS, a subnet can be thought of as a partition of the entire VPC network where you group your network resources based on your security and operational needs. Each subnet you create is associated with a Route Table, which controls the traffic going in and out of the network.

Also, when you create a subnet, you specify the CIDR block for the subnet, which is a subset of the VPC CIDR block. Each subnet must be associated with a route table, which controls the traffic to and from the subnet. If a subnet's traffic is not explicitly allowed to the Internet, it won't be.

Let's denote the total number of IP addresses under a VPC as N. The VPC CIDR block can have any value from /28 (with 16 IP addresses) to /16 (with 65,536 IP addresses) IPv4 CIDR block.

This implies that if you have a CIDR block of /20 which is equivalent to 4096 IP addresses (we get by using $N = 2^{(32-20)}$), you can create smaller subnets within this block.

For example, you could create four /22 CIDR blocks (each with 1024 IP addresses calculated using $N = 2^{(32-22)}$), or eight /23 CIDR blocks (each with 512 IP addresses calculated using $N = 2^{(32-23)}$).

Also, note that the first four IP addresses and the last IP address in each subnet CIDR block are not available for you to use, and cannot be assigned to an instance.

In terms of a graphical representation, imagine a VPC as a large rectangle representing the /20 CIDR block. Inside this large rectangle are smaller rectangles, which represent the /22 (say) CIDR blocks. Each of these smaller rectangles is a unique subnet within the AWS VPC.

AWS also allows for network ACLs or Access Control Lists to provide a rule-based routing policy for both outgoing and incoming traffic at the subnet level. They are stateless, meaning you have to have rules for both outgoing and incoming rules.

I hope this gives a good overview of how subnets work within AWS. They play a very significant role in optimizing and securing your cloud resources.

How can a NAT gateway or a NAT instance be used to secure a network in AWS?

A NAT (Network Address Translation) gateway or a NAT instance is a part of Amazon Web Services (AWS) that provides instances in a private network the option to connect to the internet or other AWS services, but prevents the internet from initiating a connection with those instances. They are therefore essential for securing a network in AWS as they help enhance the privacy and security of your private networks against unauthorized access.

A NAT device forwards traffic from the instances in the private subnet to the internet or other AWS services, and then sends the response back to the instances. This means, the instances in the private subnet can initiate outbound IPv4 traffic to the internet or other AWS services, but other devices on the internet cannot initiate connections to the instances.

To elaborate on this, consider the following;

Suppose we have two hosts A and B. Host A is on a private network and its actual (= private) IP address is '192.168.0.5'. Host B is anywhere on the Internet. Host A wants to send a packet to host B. If host A sends the packet with its private IP, then host B would send the response to '192.168.0.5' which might be a completely different device in the network of host B or the packet might be dropped by any DHCP server on the way since the IP was not issued by said server.

To solve this problem, the router/interface at the exit point of the private network comes with a public IP address. In our example, let's say this address is '176.23.120.56'. When host A sends its packet to host B via the router/interface the router/interface changes the sender address of the packet from '192.168.0.5' to '176.23.120.56' (and changes the sender port to a unique port number).

This process is done by NAT in the device. This way, the server sends the response to '176.23.120.56', the router/interface receives the packet and sends it back to host A after reversing the translation process. This technique is called NAT, and the device implementing it is called NAT gateway/device.

The use of NAT devices provides an extra layer of security for private subnets as they allow outbound communication without allowing inbound traffic initiated by an external source. Thus, this can effectively prevent any unauthorized inbound access from external sources.

Here's a graphical representation of how NAT works in an AWS setting:

$$\text{Private subnet\&} \xrightarrow{\text{(NAT device)}} \text{\&Public IP space (Internet)}$$
$$(192.168.0.5)\& \xrightarrow{\text{NAT Translation}} \&(176.23.120.56)$$

Requests from private subnet&&Response from Internet

In the diagram, '(192.168.0.5)' is the private IP address within the subnet, which gets translated to '(176.23.120.56)' in public IP space to communicate with the internet. When the response is received, the NAT device does the inverse translation and forwards it to the original requesting instance.

In summary, a NAT gateway or instance serves as a wall between

AWS private networks and the public internet, allowing the instances within private subnets to interface securely with the internet for necessary services, without exposing them to unnecessary risks from unauthorized access.

What is the function of a VPC flow log?

A Virtual Private Cloud (VPC) flow log is a critical feature in AWS that allows you to capture information about the IP traffic that goes to and from network interfaces in your VPC.

With VPC Flow Logs, AWS provides a mechanism to log network traffic in your Virtual Private Cloud (VPC), including traffic that goes to and from Elastic Network Interfaces (ENIs) present in your Virtual Private Network (VPN), Network Address Translation (NAT) gateways, your VPC connection, and any traffic routed through AWS Transit gateways.

Information logged by the VPC Flow Logs includes:

- The source IP address
- The destination IP address
- Source port
- Destination port
- The protocol
- The number of packets
- Number of bytes
- Start and end time of the flow
- Action status (whether the traffic was accepted or rejected)

VPC Flow Logs data can be utilized for many use-cases, including:

- **Network troubleshooting**: Identify traffic patterns and pinpoint bottlenecks in the network.

- **Security analysis**: Detect patterns of malicious activity and identify potential security risks.

- **Compliance auditing**: Track network changes and traffic patterns over time for compliance and regulatory purposes.

The data captured can be stored in Amazon Simple Storage Service (Amazon S3), publish it to Amazon CloudWatch Logs, or send it to Amazon Kinesis Data Firehose, depending on how you plan to process and analyze the data.

Here is a typical format of an entry in a flow log record:

```
2 123456789010 eni-abc123de 172.31.16.139 172.31.16.21 20641 22 6 20 4249
1418530010 1418530070 ACCEPT OK
```

In this case,

'2' represents the version of the flow log.

'123456789010' is the AWS account ID.

'eni-abc123de' is the ID of the ENI on which the flow was recorded.

'172.31.16.139' is the source IP address.

'172.31.16.21' is the destination IP address.

'20641' is the source port; '22' is the destination port.

'6' is the IANA protocol number.

'20' represents the number of packets transferred during the capture window.

'4249' is the number of bytes transferred.

'1418530010' '1418530070' are the start and end times of the capture window.

'ACCEPT' is the action.

'OK' is the log status.

Please note that the entry provided is just an illustrative example. An actual flow log record can contain additional or slightly different information based on version and configurations.

Remember, though VPC Flow Logs provide valuable data for monitoring and securing your network, they do not capture real-time log streams for your network interfaces. There can be a lag of several minutes between the time a flow record is captured and when it's available for viewing. Additionally, flow logs do not log all IP traffic information; they don't capture packet-level details such as packet content or header information.

How can you create a private connection to a VPC using AWS Direct Connect?

AWS Direct Connect is a network service that provides a secure, dedicated connection from a premises to AWS. It bypasses the internet to provide more predictable latency and potentially better network performance compared with internet-based connections.

To create a private connection to a Virtual Private Cloud (VPC) using AWS Direct Connect, you would generally follow these steps:

1. **Request an AWS Direct Connect Connection:** In the AWS Management Console, you first request a Direct Connect connection by choosing a suitable location, port speed, and connection type. (This might be direct connect to your on-premises network, or a hosted connection via a Direct Connect Partner). AWS will provision a port for your connection at your chosen Direct Connect location.

2. **Interconnect with AWS Direct Connect:** Once your port has been provisioned, you connect to it using a cross-connect, which must be set up with your chosen data center provider.

3. **Create a Virtual Interface:** Once the cross-connect is estab-

lished, you create a Virtual Interface (VIF) in the AWS Console. This is where you specify that you want a private connection to your VPC.

4. **Link the VIF to your VPC:** Finally, you connect your VIF to a Virtual Private Gateway or Direct Connect Gateway that is associated with your VPC.

Your network would look something like this:

'On-Premises Network <– Direct Connect –> AWS Direct Connect Location <– Cross-Connect –> AWS Direct Connect Port <– VIF –> VPC'

It's also important to note that this configuration alone doesn't block public internet access from your VPC; it just sets up a route so that traffic to and from your on-premises network will use the Direct Connect link instead of the internet. If you want to make sure your VPC is not accessible from the internet, you must also adjust your VPC's security settings, such as Network ACLs and Security Groups to control inbound and outbound traffic.

How can you secure data in transit in AWS?

Securing data in transit in AWS can be ensured using various techniques and services, such as TLS encryption, VPN connections, and AWS Direct Connect.

1. **TLS Encryption**:

Transport Layer Security (TLS) is a protocol that ensures privacy between communicating applications and users on the internet. When a server and client communicate, TLS guarantees that no third party may eavesdrop on or tamper with any message. AWS has integrated usages of TLS encryption in numerous services to ensure secure data transfer in transit.

For examples, a common scenario can be client-server communication where a user-facing application is communicating with a server. That could be using HTTPS (which leverages TLS under the hood) to ensure the security of data in transit. This is essentially end-to-end encryption.

2. **VPN Connections**:

AWS also offers Virtual Private Network (VPN) connections that secure the data in transit by establishing a secure and private tunnel from your network or device to the AWS global network. Amazon offers AWS Site-to-Site VPN and AWS Client VPN.

For example, you might have a data center that needs secure connectivity with your VPC (Virtual Private Cloud) in AWS. You would establish a Site-to-Site VPN between your data center and AWS to ensure the security of data in transit.

3. **AWS Direct Connect**:

For a more consistent network experience, AWS Direct Connect makes it easy to establish a dedicated network connection from your premises to AWS. With AWS Direct Connect, we can transfer business critical data directly from our datacenter, office, or colocation environment to and from AWS bypassing the internet-facing network, incurring less threats.

Again, consider the example of your data center needing to connect with your VPC in AWS. Direct Connect makes this connection for you, and bypassing public internet pathways means you have control over the security measures from end to end.

Remember, as part of an overall security strategy, we should always adhere to AWS' best practice of applying the principle of least privilege—which restricts user access rights to the minimum necessary—to further ensure the security of our data.

Overall, securing data in transit involves a layered approach using a combination of methods, depending on the specific requirements of your use case. AWS provides a wealth of options for securing your data at all points, making it a versatile and powerful tool for maintaining the security of your online assets.

Can you discuss the concept of a perimeter security model and how AWS supports it?

A perimeter security model is a traditional approach to network security where defenses are put mainly at the network borders and entrance points, thereby creating a "perimeter" to guard against external threats. This model follows the principle of "trust but verify" where all activities within the security boundary are "trusted" while everything outside the perimeter is considered "unverified" and thus deemed a potential threat.

In the context of traditional on-premises environment, the perimeter security model may involve firewalls, intrusion detection/prevention systems (IDS/IPS), and other similar tools. Despite this, the model has been criticized for its inadequacy in dealing with today's threat landscape where attacks can originate from within the predefined perimeter, among other issues.

On the other hand, AWS has provided mechanisms and practices that help in supporting the principles of the perimeter security model while addressing its inherent limitations.

1. **VPC (Virtual Private Cloud)**: AWS's VPC function as a virtual network layer dedicated to your AWS account. Inside a VPC, you can define your virtual network's private IP address range, create subnets, and configure security settings, thereby establishing a controllable perimeter in the AWS environment.

For instance, let's assume you configure a VPC with an IP address range 10.0.0.0/16, thereby establishing a perimeter enclosing all resources with IP addresses in this range. Now, this perimeter can be fortified by applying necessary controls at the points of interaction with the outside world.

2. **Security Groups and Network ACLs**: These are two types
of firewalls that help in controlling inbound and outbound traffic to
services and servers within your VPC. Security groups control access
at the instance level (i.e., per Amazon EC2 instance), while network
ACLs operate at the subnet level. They can be thought of as additional layers in your security perimeter that increase your control
over the flow of information into and out of your VPC.

For example, on configuring a security group to allow incoming TCP
traffic on port 22 (SSH) from source 203.0.113.1, only a client with
IP address 203.0.113.1 can establish SSH connection with your EC2
instance.

3. **AWS WAF (Web Application Firewall)**: It's a tool that you
can use to protect your web applications against common web exploits. This adds a deeper layer of control to your security perimeter,
enabling you to filter out malicious traffic before it reaches your resources.

4. **Amazon CloudFront, Amazon Route 53, and AWS Shield**:
AWS offers services like CloudFront and Route 53 to distribute traffic
to your application and mitigate potential DDoS (Distributed Denial
of Service) attacks respectively. AWS Shield adds another layer of
defense on top by providing additional DDoS protection.

Hence, while AWS supports the concept of a perimeter security model,
it also provides the options for employing a defense-in-depth strategy,
which is a modern approach to network security where layers of security are applied throughout a network. It's a more comprehensive
form of protection that defends a network at many different levels,
thereby providing alternatives whenever one mechanism fails or is
bypassed.

It's important to note that these are just part of the myriad capabilities that AWS provides for you to secure your workloads in the
cloud. Beyond these, AWS offers services and features around identity and access management (IAM), encryption, Key Management
Service (KMS), and more.

In conclusion, AWS's capabilities for network security help reinforce the principles of the perimeter security (i.e., a clear distinction between trusted and untrusted networks and the use of controls at the network edge) while at the same time facilitating a multi-layered, defense-in-depth strategy thereby addressing the model's inherent limitations.

How can you protect against Distributed Denial of Service (DDoS) attacks in AWS?

AWS provides a number of services and features to help protect against Distributed Denial of Service (DDoS) attacks. These include:

- AWS Shield: This is a managed DDoS protection service that safeguards your web applications running on AWS. AWS Shield provides automatic protections that minimize application downtime and latency, and there are no additional AWS infrastructure or maintenance costs. AWS Shield is available in two tiers: Standard and Advanced. AWS Shield Standard defends against most common DDoS attacks. If you need more advanced protection against larger and more sophisticated attacks, AWS Shield Advanced provides additional DDoS mitigation capabilities along with cost protection, and 24/7 DDoS response team (DRT) access.

- Amazon CloudFront and AWS WAF: CloudFront is a content delivery network (CDN) that can protect against network and application layer DDoS attacks by distributing traffic to points of presence around the world, thereby absorbing the impact of any attack and ensuring your application remains available. AWS WAF, a web application firewall, allows you to create custom rules that block common attack patterns, such as SQL injection or cross-site scripting (XSS), and rules that rate limit requests from individual IP addresses to protect against DDoS attacks.

- Virtual Private Cloud (VPC) security groups and network access control lists (ACLs): Using these tools, you can control inbound and

Layers	Protection Services
Layer 3/4 (Network/Transport)	AWS Shield (Standard or Advanced)
Layer 7 (Application)	AWS WAF in conjunction with AWS Shield

outbound network traffic to your AWS resources. For instance, you can limit traffic to minimize the attack surface and set up rule-based routing to help thwart DDoS attacks.

- Amazon Route 53: Route 53 is a scalable DNS and domain name registration service that can route your users to your application by translating readable domain names into the numeric IP addresses that computers can connect to. Route 53 employs various techniques to ensure high availability and resilience to DDoS attacks.

- AWS Auto Scaling: AWS Auto Scaling monitors your applications and automatically adjusts capacity to maintain steady, predictable performance at the lowest possible cost. Using Auto Scaling, it's easy to setup application scaling for multiple resources across multiple services in minutes.

Different layers of the OSI model are usually targeted by different types of DDoS attacks. Here is an example of how AWS services can protect against such attacks based on the OSI model layer that is targeted:

1. Layer 3/4 (Network/Transport): You can use AWS Shield (Standard or Advanced) for protection against volumetric and state-exhaustion DDoS attacks.

2. Layer 7 (Application): You can use AWS WAF along with AWS Shield for protection against application layer DDoS attacks.

Please note that these services should be part of a broader security strategy. It's also crucial to have an incident response plan in place in case of a DDoS attack.

The illustration below shows how different AWS services can be combined to protect against DDoS attacks:

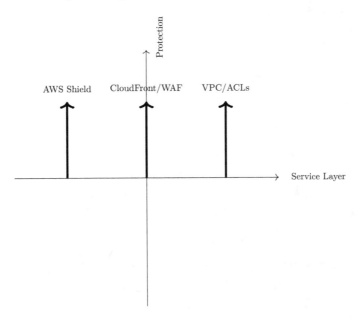

Remember to continue monitoring your applications, use AWS Cloud-Watch, AWS CloudTrail and other service level logging options for post-incident analysis and future remediation action planning.

Mathematically, DDoS attack impact can be measured and visualized by plotting number of requests over time. Algorithms like rate-based anomaly algorithms in AWS WAF can help detect and mitigate such trends. This could look like this for a rate-based anomaly (obvious spike indicating a potential DDoS):

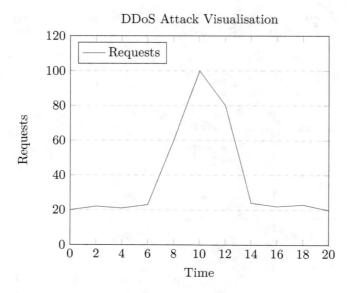

This graph represents an increase in requests during an attack period (between time 8 and 14), which is mitigated down later.

How does AWS Shield enhance network security?

AWS Shield is a managed Distributed Denial of Service (DDoS) protection service that safeguards web applications running on AWS. AWS Shield provides automatic DDoS detection and mitigation allowing applications to deliver uninterrupted performance to your users. It offers two tiers of service: AWS Shield Standard and AWS Shield Advanced.

AWS Shield Standard is designed to protect all AWS customers from common and most frequently observed DDoS attacks. It's integrated into AWS services like Route 53 (which is a scalable and highly available Domain Name System) and Cloudfront (which is a content delivery network).

AWS Shield Advanced provides advanced DDoS mitigation capabilities for more complex or larger-scale DDoS attacks. It ensures higher level of protection for your applications against DDoS attacks, and it includes cost protection, DDoS related support, threat intelligence, and integration with AWS WAF (Web Application Firewall).

Here's how AWS Shield enhances network security:

1. **DDoS Protection**: AWS Shield helps to protect your AWS applications from DDoS attacks. DDoS attacks saturate the bandwidth or resources of a target, which could be a specific application or service, making it slow or completely inaccessible for legitimate users. AWS Shield's DDoS protection mitigates this by absorbing the attack traffic at AWS edge locations, before it reaches your applications.

2. **Cost Protection**: In the event of a DDoS attack, there could be increased data transfer costs due to the large amount of inbound traffic. AWS Shield Advanced offers financial protection by covering extra data transfer costs that are incurred due to a DDoS attack.

3. **Integrated with Other AWS Services**: AWS Shield is integrated with other AWS services like Amazon CloudFront, Amazon Route 53, Elastic Load Balancer (ELB), AWS Global Accelerator, Elastic IP, and Amazon CloudWatch which provide additional layers of security.

4. **Application Level Protection**: AWS Shield Advanced provides threat intelligence and integrates with AWS WAF. This enables the service to provide an extra layer of protection against more sophisticated attacks at the application level, such as SQL injection or Cross Site Scripting (XSS).

5. **24/7 DDoS Response Team (DRT) Access**: AWS Shield Advanced users have access to the AWS DDoS response team around the clock. They can help create incident response plans, and in the event of an attack, they can help with the mitigation process.

In conclusion, AWS Shield significantly enhances network security through its robust DDoS protection, cost protection against increased data transfer costs, seamless integration with other essential AWS services, and accessibility to a dedicated DDoS response team around the clock. By leveraging AWS Shield, organisations can protect their applications from the disruption and expense of DDoS attacks, while maintaining performance and availability for their users.

4.3   Security Best Practices on AWS

What are some security best practices when using AWS?

Maintaining security is a critical aspect when utilizing cloud services. Here are several security best practices when using Amazon Web Services (AWS):

1. **Identity and Access Management (IAM):**

It is crucial to manage access to your AWS resources securely. A policy-based system can help set fine-grained access permissions for AWS resources.

- Implement least privilege access: For IAM users, roles, and groups, grant only the permission necessary to perform a task.

- Implement strong password policies: Such as minimum length, requiring a combination of letters, numbers, and non-alphanumeric characters.

- Enable multi-factor authentication (MFA) for all users.

2. **Log and Monitor Activity:**

AWS provides tools to monitor and log activities as security measures.

- For logging, use AWS CloudTrail: CloudTrail helps to track the user activity and API usage across the AWS infrastructure.

- For monitoring, use Amazon CloudWatch: CloudWatch collects monitoring and operational data in the form of logs, metrics, and events, giving a unified view of AWS resources.

- Enable VPC Flow Logs to capture information about the IP traffic going to and from network interfaces.

3. **Secure Your Applications:**

- Ensure your applications handle and store sensitive data securely.

- Regularly update and patch any application software hosted on your instances.

- Perform regular vulnerability assessments of your applications and remediate any findings.

4. **Protect data in transit and at rest:**

Use AWS services that offer encryption to protect your data.

- Protect data in transit using Secure Socket Layer (SSL) or Transport Layer Security (TLS).

- Protect data at rest using services like Amazon S3 server-side encryption, or Amazon RDS which supports encryption at rest using AWS Key Management Service.

5. **Implement a secure network architecture:**

Secure your Amazon Virtual Private Cloud (VPC) resources and use AWS best practices for distributed security.

- Use security groups and network ACLs in your VPC.

- Use Virtual Private Networks (VPN) or AWS Direct Connect to securely extend your network.

- Isolate workloads across different VPCs.

6. **Regular Audit:**

Use AWS Management and Governance tools to conduct resource configuration checks.

- Use AWS Config to assess, evaluate, and audit resource configurations.

- Use AWS Trusted Advisor to provide real-time guidance in the provision of your resources.

Remember, security in the cloud is a shared responsibility between AWS and the customer. AWS is responsible for protecting the infrastructure that runs all of the services offered in the AWS Cloud. This is commonly referred to as "security of the cloud." But customers are responsible for managing their data (including encryption options), classifying their assets, and using IAM tools to apply the appropriate permissions. This is considered "security in the cloud."

How can you protect sensitive data at rest in AWS?

AWS provides a range of data protection options to support encrypting data at rest. The use of encryption keys and access controls provides a robust method of ensuring that sensitive data is protected. Here are few ways you can protect sensitive data at rest:

1. **AWS Key Management Service (KMS)**: AWS KMS allows to create, manage, and automatically rotate encryption keys that are used to encrypt data in AWS services and within applications.

2. **AWS CloudHSM**: Use this service if you require keys to remain within a hardware security module, or if your industry regulations and standards call for this method of key storage.

3. **Amazon S3 server-side encryption**: You can also request that Amazon S3 automatically encrypt data at the object level upon upload, or you can choose to manually handle the process yourself.

4. **Amazon RDS Encryption**: You can protect your data at rest in the DB instance, its automated backups, read replicas, and snapshots.

5. **Amazon EBS encryption**: Amazon EBS encryption uses AWS Key Management Service (AWS KMS) CMKs when creating encrypted volumes and snapshots.

Here's how these services are compatible with one another in terms of encryption at rest:

Amazon S3, RDS, and EBS, all use KMS or CloudHSM to handle encryption. Any data sent to these storage solutions can be automatically encrypted at rest.

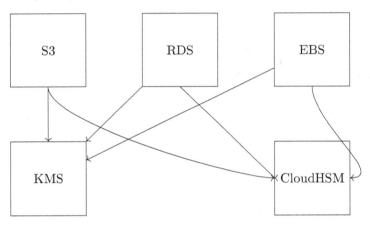

In the above chart, S3, RDS, and EBS are responsible for encrypting data at rest. They rely on KMS and CloudHSM as the mechanism for key storage and management.

Also keep these points in mind:

- Make sure to adhere to least privilege access policies while defining access to these encryption keys. Avoid sharing your keys outside your organization.

- Enable logging and monitoring to ensure no unauthorized access to sensitive data.

- In AWS it's highly recommended to use AWS KMS to manage encryption keys in order to further secure data at rest. With KMS, you do not need to worry about key management as keys are rotated and stored securely.

- Regularly review policies and access rights to ensure that they align with the current requirements of the organization.

Remember to go above and beyond to protect your data on AWS. Encrypting data at rest is just one of the things you should do, but there are many more actions you can take to secure your data in the cloud!

How can you protect sensitive data in transit in AWS?

Protecting sensitive data in transit on AWS involves methods that ensure confidentiality and integrity of data when it's being moved from one place to another. The best practices to protect your data in transit in AWS include using secure protocols, applying encryption, using AWS Certificate Manager to handle SSL/TLS certificates, and employing the AWS VPN services for secure connections.

1. **Use Secure Protocols:** Always use secure versions of the communication protocols when transmitting data. For example, use HTTPS instead of HTTP, and use SFTP or FTPS instead of FTP. AWS services such as Amazon S3, Amazon RDS, and Amazon DynamoDB natively support secure protocols, making it easier for developers to protect data in transit.

2. **Encryption in Transit:** AWS uses industry-standard transport protocols between user devices and AWS, and between AWS services. For example, AWS uses Secure Sockets Layer (SSL) and Transport Layer Security (TLS) for the secure transfer of data to and from AWS resources. It also supports the latest version of Internet Protocol

(IPv6), which includes built-in encryption for all traffic.

3. **AWS Certificate Manager (ACM):** AWS provides the AWS Certificate Manager (ACM) to handle SSL/TLS certificates which are used to identify and authenticate the parties involved in data transit. ACM can provision, deploy, and renew SSL/TLS certificates, and there is no extra cost for using this service.

4. **AWS VPN Service:** There is also the AWS VPN service, which you can use to establish a secure and private tunnel from your network or device to the AWS global network. This service is useful when you need to establish a secure connection between your on-premises network and your VPCs on AWS.

Here is a tabular summary:

Best Practices	Description
Use Secure Protocols	Always choose protocols such as HTTPS, SFTP, FTPS over HTTP, FTP.
Encryption in Transit	Use SSL/TLS for secure transfer of data to and from AWS resources.
AWS Certificate Manager (ACM)	Handle SSL/TLS certificates necessary for authentication during data transit.
AWS VPN Service	Establish secure and private tunnels from your network or device to the AWS global network.

Table 4.1: Best Practices and Descriptions

How does the Shared Responsibility Model apply to AWS security?

In AWS, security and compliance are shared responsibilities between AWS and the customer. This shared model can reduce a user's operational burden as AWS handles security 'of' the cloud, while security 'in' the cloud is the responsibility of the customer.

AWS distinguishes between security measures it provides 'of the cloud', such as protecting the infrastructure that runs AWS services, and 'in the cloud', which includes how the customer determines to configure and utilize AWS services, software, and systems.

AWS Responsibilities (Security 'OF' the Cloud): AWS is responsible for protecting the infrastructure which includes: software, hardware, networking, and facilities that run AWS Cloud services. AWS is responsible for the security configuration of its products that are considered managed services such as Amazon DynamoDB, Amazon RDS, Amazon Redshift, Amazon WorkSpaces, and others. Here, AWS handles all the tasks related to patch management, antivirus, IDS/IPS, etc.

Customer Responsibilities (Security 'IN' the Cloud): The customer's responsibility depends upon the AWS services that the customer selects. This determines the amount of configuration work the customer must perform within those services. For instance, AWS provides database services like RDS (managed) or EC2 where you install and manage your own database (unmanaged). While RDS services require less management from the customer, using EC2 for your database will require all patching and security to be managed by the customer.

By understanding and aligning with the Shared Responsibility Model, customers can ensure they're adequately protecting their data while leveraging the security benefits provided by AWS. To further ensure secure running of applications, AWS provides services such as Identity and Access Management (IAM), Virtual Private Cloud (VPC), and AWS Key Management Service (KMS). Customers can also leverage AWS security services, architectural best practices, and other resources available to enhance the security of their cloud environment.

How can you monitor security on AWS?

Monitoring security on AWS involves being able to observe, alarm, and react to changes in your AWS environment. AWS provides various tools and features to help you achieve this. However, it is essential to use a combination of these services to develop a comprehensive and robust security posture. In order to monitor security effectively on AWS, you can use the following methods:

1. **AWS CloudTrail**: AWS CloudTrail allows you to monitor API call activity on your account. AWS CloudTrail records these calls, including the identity of the API caller, the time of the call, the source IP address of the caller, the request parameters, and the response elements returned by the AWS service. This recorded information will help you keep track of changes to your AWS resources and troubleshoot operational issues.

2. **AWS Config**: AWS Config provides a detailed inventory of your AWS resources and configuration, and continuously records configuration changes. This allows you to evaluate these configurations and changes for compliance with ideal configurations defined by AWS best practices.

3. **Amazon CloudWatch**: Amazon CloudWatch is a monitoring and observability service. CloudWatch provides you with data and actionable insights to monitor your applications, understand and respond to system-wide performance changes, optimize resource utilization, and get a unified view of operational health.

4. **GuardDuty**: AWS GuardDuty is a threat-detection service which continuously monitors for malicious or unauthorized behavior that could indicate a security incident or compromise. GuardDuty identifies unusual behavior such as unexpected and possibly unauthorized infrastructure deployments, unusual API calls or potentially unauthorized deployments that indicate potentially compromised instances.

5. **Amazon Inspector**: Amazon Inspector is an automated security assessment service that helps improve the security and compliance of applications deployed on AWS. It assesses applications for vulnerabilities or deviations from best practices, including impacted networks, systems, and attached storage.

6. **Security Hub**: AWS Security Hub gives you a comprehensive

view of your high-priority security alerts and compliance status across AWS accounts.

Now, let's see how we could combine AWS services for a comprehensive monitoring strategy.

A typical use may be to have CloudTrail logs being stored in S3 bucket for archival purposes. CloudWatch alarms trigger if API calls from CloudTrail logs indicate suspicious behavior, and these triggers then notify via Amazon SNS. GuardDuty supplements this by providing threat intel on unusual API calls or potentially unauthorized deployments. AWS Config can be used in parallel to ensure that the resources are set up per best practices.

Here is an example diagram below for a comprehensive security monitoring setup:

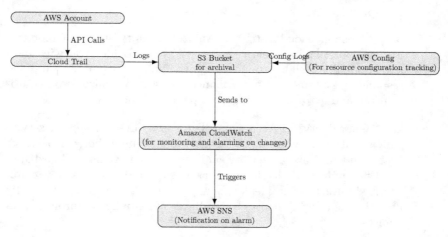

There is no one-size-fits-all answer to this question as the specifics will differ based on industry, organization size, existing security infrastructure, and many other factors. However, the above-mentioned tools will provide a solid basis for any AWS security monitoring setup.

Can you discuss some best practices for incident response on AWS?

Incident response is a key aspect for maintaining the security and integrity of your AWS resources. Here are some best practices to follow regarding incident response:

1. Configuration Management and Automation: AWS offers services such as AWS CloudFormation, AWS OpsWorks, AWS Config, and AWS Systems Manager that allow you to manage your security configurations at scale and respond to security events. They enable you to script and automate your deployment and remediation processes to avoid manual errors and reduce the time it takes to remediate an incident. You should utilize these services proactively to ensure that your environment maintains a secure state.

2. Centralize and Secure Log Storage: All security relevant events should be logged and the logs should be moved off the system and aggregated to a central location. AWS CloudTrail and Amazon CloudWatch Logs provide such capabilities. AWS even provides encryption for data at rest and in transit, helping you to meet your encryption and secure data storage requirements.

3. Implement Incident Response Playbooks: You should consider common incidents that you're likely to encounter in AWS environment and create runbooks or playbooks. These guide day-to-day operations and allow your security team to react effectively and consistently during an incident.

4. Use AWS Security Automation: AWS provides managed services like AWS Lambda, AWS Step Functions, and AWS Systems Manager Automation to automate repeatable and predictable processes.

5. Harden AWS Accounts and Services: Apply least privilege access policy to your resources and consider using AWS services like AWS GuardDuty, Amazon Macie, and AWS Security Hub to monitor your environment's security.

6. Communication During Incident Response: Communication is critical during an incident. AWS provides tools like AWS Chatbot and Amazon Chime for effective communication.

Here's a simplified example of incident response pipeline,

"Detection"   (AWS CloudTrail, AWS Config, AWS Security Hub)
↓
"Triage"   (Amazon CloudWatch Events, AWS Step Functions)
↓
"Investigation"   (Amazon Athena, Amazon QuickSight)
↓
"Remediation"   (AWS Systems Manager, AWS Lambda)

In this pipeline, each incident follows the path from detection, to triage, and then to investigation and remediation. AWS security services are used at each step to automate and streamline the process.

How can you prevent unauthorized access to your AWS resources?

Preventing unauthorized access to your AWS resources requires a comprehensive strategy that encompasses AWS Identity & Access Management (IAM), Multi-Factor Authentication (MFA), and secure design principles. Here are key best practices:

1. **Least Privilege Principle**: Provide your users the minimum levels of access or permissions they need to perform their functions. By doing this, you can limit the actions that can be performed with each IAM access key, reducing the potential damage in the event of key misuse or compromise.

2. **MFA (Multi-Factor Authentication)**: To add an extra level of protection against unauthorized access, implement MFA. MFA requires that users present two separate forms of identification (their

password and a physical or virtual MFA device).

3. **AWS IAM**: By using IAM, you can securely control access to AWS services and resources for your users. It grants granular permissions which provide control over interactions with resources in the AWS ecosystem.

4. **AWS Security Groups and NACLs**: Secure EC2 instances by only allowing trusted and necessary IP addresses to access your resources, making your resources harder to find and access by unauthorized parties.

5. **AWS Key Management Service (KMS)**: You can use KMS to create and manage cryptographic keys and control their use across a wide range of AWS services and in your applications.

6. **Enforce Strong Password Policies**: Requiring complex, lengthy passwords makes it harder for unauthorized individuals to guess or crack your users' credentials.

7. **User Activity Monitoring**: Using services like AWS Cloud-Trail, you can monitor API calls for your account, including calls made via the AWS Management Console, AWS SDKs, command line tools, and higher-level AWS services. This can help you to detect unauthorized or anomalous behavior.

8. **Auditing and Compliance**: Regularly perform audits of your environment using AWS Config and AWS Security Hub to ensure your security measures are functioning as expected, and that you are in compliance with any regulations that apply to your business.

For example, the representation of least privilege principle in 'IAM Policy' can be given as:

```
{
  "Version": "2012-10-17",
  "Statement": [
    {
      "Sid": "VisualEditor0",
      "Effect": "Allow",
      "Action": [
        "ec2:StartInstances",
```

```
      "ec2:StopInstances"
    ],
    "Resource": "arn:aws:ec2:us-east-1:123456789012:instance/*",
    "Condition": {
      "StringEquals": {
        "aws:username": "ec2-user"
      }
    }
  }
 ]
}
```

The user, 'ec2-user', is given limited permissions to start and stop instances and no other actions such as terminate or reboot.

These are some strategies to keep AWS resources secure. Remember that security is an ongoing process and should be reviewed regularly.

What are some best practices for identity and access management on AWS?

Identity and Access Management (IAM) is a crucial aspect of AWS security. Here are some best practices to follow:

1. **Least Privilege Principle**: IAM users and resources should only have the minimum permissions necessary to fulfill their role. This reduces the potential for accidental or malicious misuse of permissions.

2. **Use IAM Groups**: If several users perform the same job and need the same permissions, create an IAM group with those permissions and add the respective users to that group. This not only reduces management work but also centralizes access control.

3. **Use IAM Roles**: Instead of sharing security credentials, you should delegate permissions using IAM roles. An IAM role is an entity with defined permissions that trusted entities (like AWS services, users, or even applications) can assume.

4. **Use Multi-Factor Authentication (MFA)**: This adds an extra layer of protection by requiring two types of identification. AWS

supports virtual or hardware MFA devices.

5. **Regularly Rotate Security Credentials**: Old credentials can pose a security risk. Regularly changing credentials helps to mitigate this risk.

6. **Restrict root user access**: The root user has full access to all resources in your AWS account, which can cause significant damage if misused. It's better to use IAM users and restrict the root's usage.

7. **Use strong password policy**: A robust password policy ensures the integrity of your users' accounts. It should include things like minimum password length, requiring special characters, and regular password rotation.

8. **Audit regularly**: Utilize AWS' CloudTrail to log, continuously monitor, and maintain records of all IAM and AWS Management Console actions related to security, auditing, compliance.

Remember, IAM best practices are an essential part of overall security, but they're just one part. Networking, data encryption, monitoring and logging, regular audits, and vulnerability scanning all play crucial roles as well.

How can you ensure secure interactions between microservices in a complex AWS application?

Assuring secure interactions between microservices in an AWS application is critical and involves a layered security approach. Here, we'll offer four steps to achieve this:

1. Use VPC for Network Isolation: Amazon Virtual Private Cloud (Amazon VPC) allows users to provision a logically isolated portion of AWS. AWS resources can be launched in a defined virtual network, with greater control over IP addresses, subnets, routing tables, and network gateways, hence providing network isolation.

The VPC can be segregated into different Subnets for each microservice. For example:

$$\text{Microservice A} \rightarrow \text{VPC/Subnet A}$$
$$\text{Microservice B} \rightarrow \text{VPC/Subnet B}$$
$$\text{Microservice C} \rightarrow \text{VPC/Subnet C}$$

2. Implement IAM Policies: Identity and Access Management (IAM) enables managing access to AWS services and resources in a secure manner. IAM roles can be attached to EC2 instances hosting the microservices, thereby providing them with permissions to make API calls to other AWS services.

Let's say we have three Microservices: A, B, and C. Their IAM roles can be defined as:

   Microservice A $\rightarrow$ IAM role A (with specific permissions)
   Microservice B $\rightarrow$ IAM role B (with specific permissions)
   Microservice C $\rightarrow$ IAM role C (with specific permissions)

3. Use AWS Secrets Manager: Secrets Manager protects access to applications, services, and IT resources. This eliminates the up-front and on-going investment and maintenance costs of operating your own infrastructure for managing secrets.

4. Use AWS Shield for DDoS mitigation: AWS Shield offers managed Distributed Denial of Service (DDoS) protection.

5. Implement AWS WAF: AWS Web Application Firewall (WAF) helps protect against common web exploits.

Besides these four broad steps, it is also essential to regularly monitor and review AWS CloudTrail and AWS CloudWatch logs for any potential security threats or irregularities. This should ideally include constantly monitoring the ingress and egress data separately for each service.

Again, every architecture and application is unique; hence these are general guidelines and should be adapted based on specific needs of the application. The idea is to follow the principle of least privilege allowing only what is necessary and no more.

How can you protect against common security threats such as SQL Injection or Cross-Site Scripting (XSS) in an AWS environment?

Protecting against security threats like SQL Injection and Cross-Site Scripting (XSS) calls for a comprehensive strategy that emphasizes security at every single layer. AWS gives several services and best practices for security that can be applied. This document discusses some steps to help protect against these common security threats on AWS.

1. **Input Validation**: Always validate user input to ensure that only properly formed data is entering your workflow in your AWS environment. AWS WAF (Web Application Firewall) can help here and offers SQL injection and XSS match conditions to block such request.

2. **Use Parameterized Queries**: One way to prevent SQL injection attacks is by using parameterized queries, which can ensure that parameters (values inputted by the user) are automatically treated as literal strings, not part of the SQL command. AWS services such as Amazon RDS or DynamoDB use parameterized queries.

3. **Least Privilege Principle**: Restrict database access to just what's needed for the application to function and nothing more. With AWS, IAM policies can adhere to the 'least privilege' principle.

4. **Secure Your Environment**: Use AWS Shield for DDoS mitigation and implement AWS WAF to help protect your web applications from SQL Injection and XSS attacks.

5. **Encrypt Data**: Encrypt sensitive data in transit and at rest

using services like AWS Key Management Service (KMS).

6. **Regularly Update and Patch Systems**: Regularly patch and update your systems, maintaining the latest AWS SDKs and CLIs.

7. **Monitor and Audit**: Services such as AWS CloudTrail, AWS Config, CloudWatch logs allow you to monitor API calls, log data and have a complete audit trail. Utilizing AWS Trusted Advisor will also help optimize the security of your AWS environment.

8. **Implement Multi-Factor Authentication (MFA)**: AWS enables implementing MFA for IAM users, which gives an extra layer of protection.

9. **Cross-Site Scripting Protection**: For XSS attacks, it's important that you never trust user input and always encode input from users that are later sent to a web client. You can use Content Security Policy (CSP), which is a computer security standard introduced to prevent XSS attacks.

For example, you can use AWS WAF to create a rule that blocks common patterns of XSS attacks. AWS WAF allows you to create rules that identify patterns like the following:

S*XSS*Y

This can be blocked in AWS WAF by using the string matching conditions combined with logical AND statements. This matches the string of characters S, followed by any number of characters, followed by XSS, followed by any number of additional characters, and finishes with Y.

Please note that it's important to implement security at all layers and consider a defense in depth security strategy to minimize risks and vulnerabilities. AWS Well-Architected Framework provides a set of questions you can use to evaluate how well an architecture is aligned to AWS best practices, one of the pillars being Security.